Where History and Innovation Intersect

We hope you will enjoy this look at Boston's past and present. While we continue to evolve and grow as a global asset manager, we are proud that our roots started here. Our home town will always be an important part of our history, brand and identity.

Bart A. Grenier

Bart A. Grenier
Chairman, Chief Executive Officer and Chief Investment Officer

THE BOSTON COMPANY

ASSET MANAGEMENT, LLC

➤ A BNY MELLON COMPANY℠

BOSTON
THEN & NOW

BOSTON
THEN & NOW

PATRICK L. KENNEDY

THUNDER BAY
P·R·E·S·S

San Diego, California

Thunder Bay Press
An imprint of the Baker & Taylor Publishing Group
10350 Barnes Canyon Road, San Diego, CA 92121
www.thunderbaybooks.com

Produced by Salamander Books,
an imprint of Anova Books Ltd.
10 Southcombe Street, London W14 0RA, UK

All notations of errors or omissions should be addressed to Thunder Bay Press,
Editorial Department, at the above address. All other correspondence (author
inquiries, permissions) concerning the content of this book should be addressed
to Salamander Books, 10 Southcombe Street, London W14 0RA, UK.

Library of Congress Cataloging-in-Publication Data

Kennedy, Patrick L.
  Boston then & now / Patrick L. Kennedy.
    p. cm.
  Rev. ed. of: Boston then & now / Elizabeth McNulty. 1999.
  ISBN-13: 978-1-59223-963-4
  ISBN-10: 1-59223-963-3
  1. Boston (Mass.)--Pictorial works. 2. Boston (Mass.)--History--
Pictorial works. I. McNulty, Elizabeth, 1971- Boston then & now. II.
Title. III. Title: Boston then and now.
  F73.37.M38 2009
  974.4'6100222--dc22
                                                  2008042429

2 3 4 5 6 17 16 15 14 13

Printed in China.

ACKNOWLEDGMENTS

Andrea Baird sustained me with her love and support as I worked on this book. My father, Larry Kennedy,
suggested I take on the project to begin with, and of course he inspired me early with an interest in Boston
and history, and provided an important experience when he enlisted my aid as he updated Walter Muir
Whitehill's *Boston: A Topographical History* in 1999. That and his own work *Planning the City Upon a Hill*
were invaluable here. My mother, Judy, and brother, Paul, chipped in with feedback and moral support.
Jean Keith and my colleagues at Boston University indulged me while I divided my attention to complete
this task. Frank Hopkinson took a chance on a new author, and David Salmo worked tirelessly to bring
this book into being. For their time and assistance I am also indebted to, at minimum, Tom O'Connor,
Michael Southworth, John Avault, Ann Louise McLaughlin, Aaron Schmidt, Nicole DeLaria, Anne
Vosikas, Jeanne Gamble, Andrea Taaffe, Tim Cutter, Whitney Fox, Janine Fondon, Rodnell Collins,
Ellen Lipsey, and Adele Barbato. In addition to the sources mentioned inside and above, credit is due
to the work of Nancy Seasholes, Donlyn Lyndon, John Harris, Francis Drake, Anthony Sammarco, Peter
Vanderwarker, Richard Barrett, Eric Enders, Charles Swift, Mike Miliard, Emily Sweeney (and too many
other *Boston Globe* reporters to list), Peter F. Stevens, Chris Lovett, Gerald Gamm, Michael Greer, and
William Marchione.

PICTURE CREDITS

The publisher wishes to thank the following for kindly supplying the photographs that appear in this book:

"Then" photographs:
All "Then" images in this book were supplied courtesy of The Bostonian Society/Old State House, except
for the following pages: 8, 48, 50, 56, 60, 64, 76, 90, 92, 100, 106 main, 108, 112, 116 inset, 118, 128, 130,
132, 134, 136, 140 (courtesy of Boston Public Library); 36 (Time & Life Pictures/Getty Images); 96, 102,
104, 110, 120, 126, 142 (courtesy of Historic New England); 122 (courtesy of Shirley-Eustis House
Association); 124 (courtesy of Rodnell Collins); 138 (courtesy of D. J. Cutter & Co.).

"Now" photographs:
All "Now" images were taken by David Watts (© Anova Image Library) except for the following pages:
7 inset, 41, 47, 101, 103, 139 (Patrick L. Kennedy); 99 (Whitney J. Fox).

Anova Books is committed to respecting the intellectual property rights of others. We have therefore taken
all reasonable efforts to ensure that the reproduction of all content on these pages is done with the full
consent of copyright owners. If you are aware of any unintentional omissions, please contact the company
directly so that any necessary corrections may be made for future editions.

INTRODUCTION

Ship after ship of English Puritans landed up and down the coast of the Massachusetts Bay Colony in the 1620s and 1630s, when the region's recorded history begins. After brief stays at Salem and Charlestown, John Winthrop and his followers settled on an isolated 500-acre peninsula, really a trio of drumlins (hills of gravel left by a glacier 10,000 years ago) surrounded by salt marshes and tidal flats, and connected to the mainland by a narrow land bridge at its southern tip. Here, Boston was born.

The town grew to prominence as a seaport. By 1690 its population was 7,000. After another half-century, there were 17,000 people on the peninsula, making Boston the largest community in the American colonies.

It was a hard life for the inhabitants of Boston. Religious dissenters were banished, or sometimes worse. Most of the buildings were wood, and fires swept through town repeatedly. But as Puritan influence waned and builders discovered brick, industrious Bostonians could derive some excitement from the town's rapid growth, reflected in the expansion of its shoreline as the peninsula "wharfed out" into the harbor.

To kill an urban legend: Cows did not, through aimless wandering, trample paths that turned into today's Boston streets. Rather, the peninsula's topography dictated the paths of human pedestrians (and their bovine charges) from home to pasture (the Common), church to tavern, dock to bank—*those* routes became streets (initially with names like "the Long Back Street" and "Street from the Great Draw Bridge to the Meeting House"). Most of the settlement was clustered along the North End and waterfront; the "Trimountain" that would become Beacon Hill was still an unpeopled wild.

After the American Revolution, that settlement became inadequate indeed. Boston's population tripled, from about 18,300 in 1790 to 58,300 in 1825. Town meetings gave way to a city charter, with a mayor and selectmen drawn largely from Boston's merchant class. Speculators engineered the leveling of the three hills (only Mount Vernon, now Beacon Hill, remains, sixty feet shorter than it was) and the filling in of Boston's coves and inlets.

New neighborhoods were laid out in grid patterns, but separately, at different times, and in varying sizes, surrounding the colonial-era central district. That explains the apparently jumbled patchwork of streets that bedevils tourists and even locals today. (It does not, however, explain the city's mystifying scarcity of street signage.)

Of course, much of this development took place before photography, so we must visualize the era using written accounts and drawings. But beginning with the era of heavy industrialization in the mid-nineteenth century, we can see Boston as it was, albeit in black and white.

These pictures include some of the aging seventeenth-century structures that were—or seemed—destined for demolition. (Thanks to a preservation movement in the early twentieth century, many of those old buildings are still with us today.) It also includes early morning views of the brand-new neighborhoods in the Back Bay, South End, and South Cove. (The first photographers preferred to avoid busy streets because long exposures turned horses and people into blurs.)

Without question, Ireland's Great Famine in the 1840s altered the course of Boston's history. By 1856, 130,000 Irish refugees had come through Boston Harbor, many settling in the crowded North End, the city's original residential neighborhood. Boston's landfilling and building projects drew on the new supply of unskilled laborers. Those immigrants' descendants eventually came to dominate the city—and one, John F. Kennedy, would become president of the United States.

But Boston's story is not simply one of Yankees supplanted by Irish. From its beginning and into the present, the city has been affected by waves of Protestant French Huguenots, African Americans, Scottish Canadians, Sicilians and Neapolitans, Azoreans, Russian Jews, Cape Verdeans, Haitians, Vietnamese, Cambodians, Greeks, and Lithuanians—to name a few.

The progressing population boom begat another major development. Between 1868 and 1874, five bordering towns were annexed to Boston: Charlestown, Brighton, West Roxbury, Roxbury, and Dorchester. South Boston and East Boston had already been annexed, and Hyde Park would follow in 1912. A rapid transit network shortened travel time and allowed for commuting between the busy downtown and (initially) pastoral hometowns. The traditional rural routes became commercial arteries served by streetcars, and new streets were laid out among them, filling with triple-decker homes for the newer ethnic arrivals. Taken together, those neighborhoods—each with their own stories and strong identities—compose most, by far, of the City of Boston's current forty-six square miles and roughly 600,000 people.

To paraphrase the narrator in E. L. Doctorow's *The Waterworks*, the citizens of yesteryear did not go about their business as if they were merely laying the groundwork for our modern world. Nevertheless, some visionaries certainly had the city's future health and success in mind. The legacy of Charles Bulfinch and Frederick Law Olmsted, among others, endures in some of the city's finest buildings and parks.

Inevitably, the powerful have also made mistakes. In the mid-twentieth century, when Boston was long past its prime as a port, it seemed desperate measures were required to produce flows of automobile traffic and investment dollars, even if it meant evicting people and demolishing their homes. Today, the results look desperate.

However, having learned a hard lesson or two, Boston quickly became a model of smart revitalization and inclusive planning. The hope now is that its biggest new area of potential, the swath of open land left by the depressing of the Central Artery, will see similarly thoughtful progress in the decades to come.

Boston has a rare combination of vitality and innovation with a healthy sense of heritage and history. It is made up of the thousands of daily decisions by—and interactions among—a more diverse and peaceable cross-section of folk than the city often gets credit for. Bostonians work, study, drink, eat, root, and celebrate in different ways, but really, it's not such a big town, and we're all in it together.

For two centuries, herds of cattle and flocks of sheep grazed on the verdant pastures of privately owned Noddles Island, northeasterly across the harbor from Boston. Then, in 1833, General William H. Sumner bought out his relatives and formed the East Boston Company to develop the 660-acre island as a residential and commercial district. The company leveled hills, filled in marshes, laid out streets, and started a ferry service, and in just two decades, East Boston's population exploded from just eight people to 15,000. Many of the new residents were Canadian and Irish immigrants who worked in the island's maritime industries. Here, Donald McKay lived and maintained a shipbuilding concern; McKay designed the *Flying Cloud*, the clipper ship that broke records with its voyage around Cape Horn. Still, as late as 1860, when this photo was taken, neighboring Hog Island remained relatively undeveloped. From its grassy heights, looking toward Charlestown and Boston, the Bunker Hill Monument is faintly visible on the horizon.

More immigrants—first Eastern European Jews, then predominantly Italians—necessitated more housing. Streets were laid out on Hog (later Breed's) Island in the 1890s, although the grid pattern used on Noddles faltered here at the hilly terrain of Orient Heights. With more marsh filling, the two islands became one East Boston, or "Eastie." Eventually, four tunnels were built connecting Eastie to Boston. In the 1960s, Logan International Airport (far left) expanded by filling in the flats and enveloping three more islands—Bird, Governors, and Apple—

and unfortunately obliterating a popular public park designed by Frederick Law Olmsted on Wood Island. Today, maritime manufacturing has almost disappeared from East Boston, although a major supplier of peacoats to the U.S. Navy is still located here. The most recent arrivals to this diverse neighborhood are Latin American and Asian immigrants. Realtors have also enticed young professionals, even attempting to rebrand Eastie as "EaBo" in the 1990s. This photo was taken from the landmark Madonna Shrine in Orient Heights (inset).

First launched in 1797, the *Constitution* was one of the original six ships that made up the early U.S. Navy. Maine pine and Georgia oak composed the forty-four-gun warship's exceptionally sturdy hull and towering masts. (The main mast rises 220 feet, just a foot shy of the nearby Bunker Hill Monument.) Paul Revere coated the ship's bottom with copper. Early on, the *Constitution* sailed against pirates in the Mediterranean, but the vessel earned its tough reputation and nickname, "Old Ironsides," in the War of 1812. In particular, she defeated the HMS *Guerriere*, until then the pride of the powerful British navy. All told, Old Ironsides went undefeated in forty-two battles. Thrice between 1830 and 1930, talk arose of scrapping the aging ship or using it for target practice. Each time, public sentiment and powerful defenders arose to salvage and repair the docked symbol of national pride. Shown here in 1931, the *Constitution* is about to take to sea for the first time in thirty-four years.

The *Constitution* is still docked at the Charlestown Navy Yard, which built and serviced ships for the navy for 174 years. The eighty-four-acre yard on the Mystic River produced almost all of the navy's rope, and its Chain Forge and Foundry invented die-link chain. During World War II, the Navy Yard employed 47,000 workers. The yard declined in peacetime, decommissioning in 1974. The bulk of the area was redeveloped, with offices and condos replacing the warehouses and foundries in the 1980s. But the Navy Yard remains as Boston's most-visited site. It includes an 1832 pump house, opened as a museum in 1976 and renovated in 1992, as well as a World War II destroyer, the USS *Cassin Young*. Naturally, the main attraction is still Old Ironsides, today the world's oldest fully commissioned warship. Of course, she doesn't see much action nowadays—just a few turnarounds in Boston Harbor during the summer—most notably on the Fourth of July.

The 1775 battle that the Bunker Hill Monument commemorates was devastating: nearly half the victorious British regiment was wounded or killed, and Charlestown was burned to the ground. However, the Americans' first pitched battle with the King's Army was a psychic boost to the revolutionary cause. Eight years later, with the war won, Charlestown began rebuilding. In 1825 construction began on the 221-foot Egyptian Revival granite obelisk at the top of Breed's Hill (where the battle was actually fought). Seventeen years later—thanks in part to a weeklong bake sale—it was completed. By the mid-twentieth century, the Irish Americans who had come to dominate Charlestown continued to celebrate Bunker Hill Day (June 17), and its neighborhood pride, with a parade up Monument Avenue. John F. Kennedy would march in it as the district's representative in Congress and a member of the Bunker Hill Council of the Knights of Columbus. Monument Avenue is seen here in 1964—not long after Kennedy's assassination.

A Canadian travel writer in 1982 commented that Charlestown was "a sleepy suburb that retains the air of an eighteenth-century town" and that it looked more like "a European village" than an urban American neighborhood. "The houses are decorated with brass door knockers, and gay window boxes full of flowers." Indeed, Charlestown is packed with attractive Federal-style frame houses. (Not surprising, since the entire peninsula had to be rebuilt from scratch after the Revolution.) What the travel writer couldn't see, however, was a working-class neighborhood beginning to gentrify. Having long since ousted the Yankees from their last refuge at Monument Square, the Irish "Townies" themselves felt threatened by demographic changes—first from desegregation efforts in public schools and housing in the 1970s and 1980s, then from waves of young professionals buying up homes along charming streets like Monument Avenue. Nevertheless, the disparate residents of today's Charlestown have largely learned to coexist—and all embrace the monument as a symbol of their shared, adopted town heritage.

It is 224 steps to the top of the Bunker Hill Monument, where one is rewarded with one of the best vistas in Boston. In this 1960s view, the tallest buildings are: at left, the Custom House Tower, State Street Bank, and the Art Deco New England Telephone Building; and at right, the JFK, Suffolk County Courthouse, and Saltonstall buildings. Downtown Boston's proximity to Charlestown fueled what author J. Anthony Lukas called the neighborhood's favorite sport in the 1930s: looping. A youth would venture downtown, steal a car, roar through City Square, pass the police station, and lead cops on a chase up to Bunker Hill Street and back, completing a "loop" to the cheers of hundreds of spectators lining the streets. Legend has it that Paul Revere once "borrowed" Charlestown resident John Larkin's horse, never to return it. Perhaps later Townies were settling the score by taking a proper Bostonian's wheels.

With a wider lens, we see not only the office towers—too numerous to list here—of the Financial District, but also the Hancock, Prudential, and other buildings along the Back Bay (at right). Beneath the golden dome of the State House, the big arena is the TD Banknorth Garden, and to its right is the Leonard P. Zakim Bunker Hill Bridge. The unwieldy name of the world's widest cable-stayed bridge represents a compromise honoring both a civil-rights activist and the monument echoed in its design. The grain elevator and Interstate 93 interchange are gone. The church on Warren Street is St.

Mary's. On that site in the 1600s sat the thatched house of the peninsula's first European settler, Thomas Walford. Charlestown's first Roman Catholic congregation opened a small church there in 1829, and replaced it with this granite Gothic Revival structure in 1892. Today, the neighborhood's proximity to downtown has drawn new residents who work in some of those towers across the water, where the Mystic, Charles, and Chelsea rivers meet Boston's inner harbor.

Puritans settled Charlestown—a peninsula the native Pawtuckets had called Mishawum—in 1628, two years before a group of them led by John Winthrop left for the nearby Shawmut peninsula and established Boston. By 1810 Charlestown was the third-largest town in New England. It incorporated as a city in 1847, and Charlestown's city hall opened here at the former Market Square, renamed City Square. In 1874 Charlestown voted for annexation to Boston—as did a slew of Boston's bordering towns that decade. Combining Renaissance and Romanesque revival styles, the Roughan Building was built in 1899 and housed a haberdashery, drug store, and other businesses. For decades, youth street gangs, like the Arrows and the Wildcats, held dances on the building's top floor. In 1901 the Boston Elevated Railway cut through City Square, rumbling from the northern suburbs to downtown Boston and back, and darkening a swath of the neighborhood for three generations. The square is shown here circa 1963.

City Square was the site of some unsolved murders during a mob war in the mid-1960s, and it was a run-down spot into the 1970s. Charlestown native and football Hall of Famer Howie Long recounted to *Sports Illustrated* that his father lived in a rooming house on the square. (Another sports star from the neighborhood is Jack O'Callahan, who played on the U.S. ice hockey team that upset the Soviet Union at the 1980 Olympics.) But the area was due for a revival. After lengthy and often heated negotiations between residents and the Boston Redevelopment Authority, the Charlestown segment of the elevated Orange Line, as it was now called, closed in 1975 and was torn down. Over the next twelve years, the entire Orange Line was realigned and placed belowground, while City Square went through a dramatic renewal. The Roughan Building was rehabilitated in 1985, and today it houses Olives, a very fashionable restaurant run by chef Todd English. In the foreground is the foundation for the Great House, briefly the colony's seat of government.

Figuring prominently in "Paul Revere's Ride," the poem by Henry Wadsworth Longfellow, Old North Church was built in 1723, as Puritan power waned and Boston's Anglican congregation outgrew King's Chapel. Christ Church is its official name. The landmark 197-foot steeple wasn't added until 1740; its bells were imported from England four years later. A suspected smuggler donated some of the church's interior decorations—angel statues intended for a Catholic convent in Canada, stolen from a French ship. In 1750 a second-generation French Protestant, teenager Paul Revere, was a bell-ringer for Old North Church. Twenty-five years later, sexton Robert Newman famously placed two lanterns in its steeple to warn colonists of British troop movements so that Revere and other couriers could ride the countryside to deliver the message. In 1806 a hurricane toppled the wooden steeple, which was replaced by a shorter brick tower, seen in this photo taken a century later. To the left is Copp's Hill Burying Ground, where Newman lies.

A renewed awareness of their Colonial history took hold of Bostonians in the early twentieth century, and in 1912 the Old North Church's interior was repainted white and its pews reverted to the old box style. The congregation bought the neighboring Washington Memorial Garden in 1934. Twenty years later, Hurricane Carol blew down the church's second steeple, and a wooden replica of the first steeple was raised in its place. Boston's oldest house of worship is not only a popular tourist attraction but is still an active Episcopal church, in continuous operation since its founding (except for three years during the Revolution) and today draws parishioners from among the North End's more recent arrivals. The church is also still a landmark in the neighborhood, which has retained its nineteenth-century skyline. Incidentally, Hull Street, from where these photos were taken, boasts a distinctive dwelling: a ten-foot-wide house, the narrowest in Boston.

Minister Increase Mather (father of Cotton Mather, infamous for his role in the Salem witch trials) lived on this spot until his house burned down in 1676. Four years later, merchant Robert Howard built what is now the oldest house in Boston. Silversmith and patriot Paul Revere, the son of a French Huguenot named Apollos Rivoire, bought the house in 1770. There he lived, raising fourteen children, for more than twenty years. It was a stone's toss from his cousin Nathaniel Hichborn's home, and a short walk to his workshop. Revere and his wife moved to Charter Street in the 1790s, but he didn't sell this house until 1800. Over the course of the next century, waves of immigrants washed over the North End, and Paul Revere's old place on North Square would house tenement apartments, a candy factory, a cigar factory, Banca Italiana, and by 1895, when this photo was taken, "a Hebrew green grocery shop," as it was described by a contemporary.

In 1905 preservation-minded citizens formed the Paul Revere Memorial Association, bought the property, and commissioned architect Joseph Everett Chandler to restore the house to its Colonial appearance, which included removing the third-floor addition as well as refitting the building with a steep overhanging roof, clapboard siding, and diamond-paned casement windows. The association opened the house as a museum in 1908. In 1970 they purchased Revere's cousin's former home, seen at left, sharing the Revere House's courtyard. Now part of the same museum complex, the Pierce/Hichborn House happens to be the city's first brick dwelling. The Revere House today contains fine samples of the silversmith's work, plus the saddlebags from his "midnight ride" in April 1775. North Square has also been home to Thomas Hutchinson (descendant of Anne Hutchinson, father of royal governor Thomas Hutchinson) and John F. "Honey Fitz" Fitzgerald (a mayor of Boston and grandfather of John F. Kennedy).

When renowned architect Charles Bulfinch built this church on Hanover Street in 1804, it housed the New North Congregational Society, offspring of the Puritan Old North Meeting House at North Square (not to be confused with the Anglican Old North Church across town). Paul Revere cast the copper bell hung in its belfry. The church became the Second Unitarian in 1813. Thousands of Irish began to arrive in the North End during the Great Famine of the 1840s, and the Boston archdiocese of the Roman Catholic Church bought this building in 1862, turning it into St. Stephen's. The entire building was moved back twelve feet when the street was widened in 1870. Rose Fitzgerald (mother of John F. Kennedy) was christened here in 1890, four years before this picture was taken.

Historically an Irish parish, St. Stephen's began to decline as other Catholic immigrants—mainly Portuguese and Italian—poured into the North End and founded their own parishes (such as nearby St. Leonard's, New England's first Italian-built church) and the Irish began moving on to Charlestown, South Boston, and beyond. St. Stephen's was fairly run-down by the 1960s, but the archdiocese's cardinal, Richard Cushing, led a fund-raising effort to save and restore it, which included losing the front staircase. The project earned Cushing the Boston Society of Architects' Historic Preservation Award in 1970. Today, St. Stephen's is one of the city's treasures—its only existing church built by Bulfinch. Revere's bell still hangs in the belfry, and across Hanover Street is the Paul Revere Mall, a park known hereabouts as "the Prado."

The North End's main thoroughfare was once known as "the Long Back Street." It has been home to Benjamin Franklin and Cotton Mather, among others. In the 1700s, up until relations with Mother England soured, young North Enders celebrated Guy Fawkes Day (November 5) with a "Pope's Night" procession down Hanover Street, in which they sarcastically paraded a devilish effigy of the Vatican leader, which they then burned. In the North End of the 1930s, this would have been an incredibly bad idea. After decades of immigration from Ireland, Eastern Europe, the Azores, and southern Italy and Sicily, the North End was now 99.9 percent Italian-born or -descended, according to the 1930 census. (Note the signage in this 1936 photo on a building at the corner of Hanover and Parmenter streets.) The North End was also densely packed, with 44,000 people living in less than one square mile. The processions down Hanover Street at that time were during the summer, celebrating Catholic saints' feast days.

The North End's population dropped to elbow-room levels as some returning World War II veterans went to college or moved to northern suburbs. The district lost none of its vitality, however. In her iconoclastic 1961 book *The Death and Life of Great American Cities*, Jane Jacobs deemed it "the healthiest place in the city," finding a genuine model in its safe, lively sidewalks and mixed-use buildings—shops at street level, apartments above. Of course, the North End did such a good job of "unslumming itself," as Jacobs put it, that it began to attract well-off professionals in the 1970s and 1980s. Today, its population of approximately 10,000 is no more than 40 percent Italian. But the neighborhood remains the Italian folk heart of eastern Massachusetts, drawing thousands back for its ever-popular feast days. It also has many Italian restaurants; there are thirty just on Hanover Street alone. This, however, is a corner store in the photograph. (Actually, were the sign fully phonetic, it would be "Connah Sto-ah.")

Seen here is the North End from the Custom House Tower, circa 1963. Along the right is Commercial Street, site of a surreal catastrophe in 1919, when a two-million-gallon tank of molasses burst inside the Purity Distilling Company, and a dark wave fifteen to twenty feet high surged across the street, severely damaging the elevated railway and drowning twenty people in nearby apartment buildings. Running across the bottom of this photo, the Central Artery was another sort of disaster for the North End. An elevated highway seemed like a forward-looking solution to Boston's traffic problems when it was proposed in 1930. But when the project began in the 1950s, it was painful for North Enders, as it involved property taking, evictions, and demolition. The Central Artery, or John F. Fitzgerald Expressway, opened for traffic in 1959 and rather quickly seemed a dated eyesore. It also cut off the neighborhood from the rest of the city and plagued it with noise and pollution for decades.

In many ways, the jury is still out on the Central Artery's replacement. For one thing, it will simply take time before the Rose Kennedy Greenway—so far, more a concept than a reality—blossoms. Residents, developers, and green space advocates have yet to agree on a vision, or even on whether there should be one vision, for the corridor of open land left by the highway's burrowing underground during the Big Dig (begun in 1991, completed in 2004). Also, the scandalously costly new Central Artery Tunnel has yet to prove wholly error-free; in fact, it leaks. However, there have been immediate benefits aboveground: peace and quiet. Furthermore, certain patches of the greenway already delight and attract visitors, even though the segment here seems dominated by a ramp. The park at the right, however, is unrelated. With its waterfront view, Christopher Columbus Park has been one of the city's most popular public places since it opened in 1976.

Dick "Honeyboy" Finnegan of Dorchester won the welterweight bout that christened the Boston Garden when the arena opened on Causeway Street next to North Station in 1928. A few days later, the Boston Bruins of the National Hockey League played their first game in their new home, losing 1–0 to the Montreal Canadiens. Sixteen thousand fans—at least a thousand over capacity—saw the game, many of them accessing the Garden via the convenient Boston Elevated Railway. The Bruins reigned supreme as the

Garden's main attraction throughout its history. There were also concerts, circuses, rodeos, religious meetings, professional wrestling events, and speeches by presidents and a prime minister (Winston Churchill). But after World War II, the Garden housed an additional major sports franchise, the National Basketball Association's Boston Celtics. By the time this photo was taken on Canal Street in 1964, the Celtics, coached by Red Auerbach, had already won seven championships to the Bruins' three.

In 1966 the Bruins drafted Bobby Orr. One of the greatest hockey players ever and a New England folk hero to this day, Orr led the Bruins to two more championships, in 1970 and 1972. Meanwhile, the Celtics—with stars like Bill Russell in the 1960s and Larry Bird in the 1980s—won nine more championships at the Garden. In 1995 the arena closed and a new one, called the FleetCenter, opened right next to it. (The Garden was finally demolished in 1998.) The Massachusetts Bay Transportation Authority's Green Line station here was moved underground in 2004. For more than a decade, the roomier but less raucous FleetCenter seemed to spell failure for the Bruins and the Celtics, both of whom fared poorly for long after the move. However, in 2005, the building was renamed the TD BankNorth Garden, and on June 17, 2008—hours after this photo was taken—the Celtics claimed another championship. Coincidence? Maybe.

Causeway Street runs along the line of a dam, built shortly after Boston's settlement, that created the Mill Pond out of the former marsh adjacent to the North End. As the city's population grew, so did its need for more land, and over the first two decades of the nineteeth century, Beacon Hill was leveled and the Mill Pond filled in—neither the city's first nor last such land-making project. Charles Bulfinch laid out the streets for what became known as Bulfinch Triangle. The Boston Elevated Railway opened in 1901 and included a stop at North Station. Here, across the street from the Boston Garden, in the shadow of the El, is a tavern at the corner of Causeway and Friend streets in the 1950s. The triangle was home to many such unpretentious eateries and watering holes.

Boston's last elevated rail section was finally torn down in 2004 when the North Station Green Line stop was moved underground, newly accessible to the North Station Orange Line stop. It was all part of the massive engineering effort carried out during the Big Dig, when the elevated Central Artery highway through Boston was moved underground. While they get a little more sun nowadays, Causeway and the other streets of Bulfinch Triangle are still lined with sports bars and other good places to meet before a game. As for the unsavory characters who also seem to line these streets on game days, sports historian Richard Johnson is pretty sure that more than a few of them have "sent their kids to Boston College or Harvard on the lucre reaped from scalped tickets."

When the granite Charles Street Jail opened in 1851, it was considered a significant achievement of modern prison design. Gridley J. Fox Bryant designed it with input from traveling prison reformer Reverend Louis Dwight, improving upon some elements of the penitentiaries at Auburn and Ossining ("Sing Sing") in New York. The jail's acclaimed design was the first from the United States to appear in the London periodical the *Builder*, and it was imitated for decades, including by the District of Columbia Jail. The jail's best-known inmate was future mayor and governor James Michael Curley, who served ninety days after he was caught taking a civil service exam for a friend. While inside, Curley read every book in the jail's library—and ran a successful bid for a seat on the Boston Board of Aldermen (precursor to the Boston City Council).

Along with Massachusetts General Hospital, naturally, Charles Street Jail was one of a handful of buildings to escape the bulldozing of the West End in the late 1950s. The jail closed in 1991 under a federal order. After an intensive five-year "reuse" restoration, the National Historic Landmark opened in September 2007 as the Liberty Hotel. The well-lit building contains comfortable guest rooms as well as fine dining establishments called Alibi (where the drunk tank was located) and Clink. In contrast with the meager fare the building's former denizens could expect at mealtime, patrons of Clink can munch on truffled caramel popcorn with smoked sea salt, fried green tomatoes with minted watermelon salad and Sangria reduction, and espresso-glazed short ribs with honey sherry–glazed cipollini onions. Not all of the Liberty Hotel's guest rooms are in the old jail building, however. In fact, most are in the sixteen-story tower across the courtyard, at left.

From the Custom House Tower in the 1940s, the view is to the northwest, toward the Charles River and the city of Cambridge across it. The tall building on the left is the Suffolk County Courthouse. Along the river are Suffolk County Jail and Massachusetts General Hospital, and below them is the West End. The cupola of the Old West Church (at this time the neighborhood's library branch) is visible. Below that is the wide curve of Cambridge Street, and to the right of that is the notorious and beloved nightlife district, Scollay Square. "Scollay is garish, raucous, and uninhibited, but it is not sinister," wrote one columnist of the day. "Its atmosphere is of youth and it is vividly and throbbingly alive" with theaters, taverns, and all the establishments that "Jack Ashore considers the requisites for a well-spent evening." But another wrote that the place was "mean-spirited, sour, brutish, and nasty."

The glass Citizens Bank Building at left reflects the perch, now called the Marriott Custom House Tower. The dark tower to its right is the Boston Company Building, with 60 State Street toward the center. Just to the right of center is the city hall, regarded by many as a bizarre concrete monstrosity, surrounded by Scollay Square's 1960s replacement, Government Center. The John F. Kennedy Federal Building above the city hall obscures the West End, which no longer exists. That low-rent neighborhood was razed in the late 1950s to make way for the luxury apartment buildings of Charles River Park, whose Longfellow Place is seen behind and to the right of the JFK. This was probably Boston's most controversial redevelopment project ever. Also visible, in the lower right-hand corner, is one of Boston's most successful projects, Quincy Market, which was revitalized in the 1970s to bring shoppers and tourists back into the city. Faneuil Hall, with its gold-plated cupola, can be seen behind the market.

Bounded by Beacon Hill, Bulfinch Triangle, the Charles River, and Scollay Square, the West End was once a fashionable district of large single-family homes and well-kept gardens. The Prince of Wales stayed in the Revere House hotel there in 1860. But before long, the area was built up with tenements to catch the North End's overflow of Irish immigrants. The clean-living Martin "Mahatma" Lomasney was the West End's political leader for years, first as ward boss, then state senator, city alderman, and finally state representative. This picture of South Margin Street was taken between 1886 and 1905, as the West End's makeup was shifting from Irish to Jewish and its population was reaching its peak of 23,000. After the West Church on Cambridge Street became the West End Branch of the Boston Public Library in 1894, it was known for a "fine collection of Judaica," wrote Walter Muir Whitehill.

The West End was predominantly Italian by 1930, although it was more diverse, and less cohesive, than the North End. Sociologist Herbert Gans lived in the neighborhood in the 1950s. "The West End was not a charming neighborhood of 'noble peasants,'" he wrote in his study, *The Urban Villagers*. "It was a run-down area of people struggling [with] low income, poor education." Yet "it was a good place to live," Gans added, and the "vast majority of West Enders had no desire to leave" when the city, desperate to bring back development and dollars, decided to use federal funds to bulldoze the entire neighborhood, save the hospital and a few historic structures. Scattering the approximately 10,000 residents, the project obliterated the old network of streets in 1960, replacing it with what was called Charles River Park, an isolated development of landscaping and luxury towers—like Longfellow Place, near where South Margin Street once intersected Staniford. "A scar on Boston's skyline," historian Lawrence Kennedy called it.

Called "the pepperpot bridge" for its unique towers, the Longfellow Bridge (left) replaced the 1794 West Boston Bridge as the conduit of traffic to and from Cambridge. Edmund March Wheelwright designed the 1907 bridge after a trip to St. Petersburg, Russia. From Cambridge, the 1950 Boston skyline is marked by the Suffolk County Courthouse and the golden dome of the State House on Beacon Hill. The tall spire at right belongs to the First Church, in the Back Bay. Once an actual bay, this neighborhood was created during the 1860s and 1870s with earth dug from Needham, west of here. Defending Boston's relative lack of skyscrapers, local columnist George Weston pointed to a few "at well-spaced intervals . . . just enough to show that Boston could, if she chose. These massive buildings with their setback type of construction are, in their individuality, things of great beauty—a beauty which would be entirely lost if they were crowded together."

Spotted in movies such as *Good Will Hunting*, the Longfellow today is more commonly called the "salt and pepper bridge." In the wake of a disastrous bridge collapse in Minnesota in 2007, the federal government declared the aging Longfellow Bridge off-limits for large trucks until it can be repaired. Furthermore, a tradition was suspended when pedestrians were also prohibited from the bridge during Boston's Fourth of July celebration. Normally, thousands gather on it to watch the fireworks burst over the Charles as the

Boston Pops orchestra plays the Hatch Shell on the Esplanade (the wooded park on the shore). The river itself is used entirely for recreational boating and sailing, and collegiate sculling races—including the annual Head of the Charles. Like the North End, Beacon Hill hasn't changed appreciably in appearance since the nineteenth century. The skyline beyond Beacon Hill, however, would dismay Weston.

This photograph was taken from Union Street looking down Marshall Street in 1890. Named for Boston's first settler, William Blackstone (or Blaxton), this little preserve is the oldest layout in Boston, with street names like Salt Lane, Marsh Lane, and Creek Square alluding to the area's early existence as a salt marsh with a creek running through it. The three-and-a-half-story brick structure at center was built in 1714 and added to in 1724 and again in 1830. A residence until 1742, then a dry-goods store, it became Atwood and Bacon's Oyster House in 1826. The Revolution-inclined *Massachusetts Spy* was once printed on the third floor; the revolution-adverse Louis Philippe (future French king) later lived on the second. Down narrow Marshall Street lived John Hancock's brother Ebenezer; his house became a shoe store in 1798. Union Street was once called Green Dragon Lane after its former landmark, the Green Dragon Tavern, the unofficial headquarters of the American Revolution.

Its bordering streets have been paved with asphalt, but the lovable, haphazard Blackstone Block still stands intact. Atwood and Bacon's Oyster House changed its name to Ye Olde Union Oyster House in 1916. It is today Boston's oldest restaurant (dating from its 1826 founding). In the building at left is Boston's oldest tavern, the Bell in Hand. Although it has moved a few times, the Bell in Hand has been in continuous operation since 1795, when it was opened by retired town crier James Wilson on now-forgotten Pie Alley.

The tavern moved here from Devonshire Street in 1968. The Green Dragon Tavern, today owned and run by an Irish family, now sits on still-cobblestoned Marshall Street, close to the site of its spiritual ancestor on Union Street. The shop in Ebenezer Hancock's old house closed in 1963, by which time it was the longest-running shoe store in the United States. That building today houses the law offices of Swartz & Swartz. Seen in the inset photo is the Holocaust Memorial, a new addition to Union Street.

This is the rear of Blackstone Block, where every weekend for 175 years, pushcart produce-sellers (above) have haggled with customers shopping for fresh apples, cantaloupes, tomatoes, and spinach. Blackstone Street was built over what was once the narrow creek that divided Boston from the North End. These photos show the street in the 1930s. The main picture shows the corner of Blackstone Street (left) and Hanover Street (right, fronted by Kennedy & Co.). This commercial building dates to the 1830s. Workmen digging for its foundation uncovered and restored the Boston Stone. Originally a painter's grindstone, it had been set in the wall of an eighteenth-century house once located here, to be used as a reference point when speaking of distance from Boston. Later, German immigrant and cigar-roller Frank Oberle opened the Bostonia Cigar Company in this building.

Toward the 1950s, as the block declined, the owners of most of the buildings on this side of Blackstone Street had their vacant top floors removed to reduce tax assessments. At left, the clock tower in the distance belongs to the Custom House, now a hotel. When the federal government built it in 1915, its thirty stories rose 370 feet higher than the city's 125-foot height limit. At right is Marshall Street, leading back to Ye Olde Union Oyster House on Union Street, with the 1969 skyscraper at 28 State Street rising in the distance behind it. The row of buildings on the other side of Blackstone Street are long gone, demolished in the 1950s to make way for the Central Artery, itself now gone—gone underground, that is, during the Big Dig.

The outcry raised by some traditional door-to-door merchants notwithstanding, French Huguenot Peter Faneuil built this central food market in 1742, with an upstairs hall that became Boston's town meeting space. The cupola's gold-plated grasshopper weathervane may have been inspired by a similar one on the London Royal Exchange. Faneuil Hall was remodeled in 1762 after a fire gutted the interior. Throughout that decade, men like Samuel Adams and Joseph Warren publicly railed against British policies at raucous town meetings here. In 1805 Charles Bulfinch doubled the hall in width and height, keeping the style the same. After Boston incorporated as a city in 1822, town meetings ended, but the hall still hosted rallies and debates. Abolitionists such as Frederick Douglass and William Lloyd Garrison appeared here to speak out against another kind of tyranny—slavery—in the 1840s and 1850s. The hall is seen here a decade or two later, still a center of agricultural commerce.

Seen as one descends the steps alongside city hall, across Congress Street, Faneuil Hall looks essentially the same as it has for 200 years. The statue with arms folded is Adams, and the peaked-roof tower to the right is Marketplace Center, built in the early 1980s. Faneuil Hall and Quincy Market behind it were closed to automobile traffic and trees were planted as part of the area's wildly successful renewal in the 1970s. Having continued its tradition throughout the twentieth century—Susan B. Anthony spoke here for women's suffrage—the hall still hosts political rallies, first-grade spelling bees, naturalizations of new American citizens, inductions for new lawyers to the Massachusetts Bar, and everything in between. The basement, however, runs to gift shops rather than meat stalls. On the cupola, the grasshopper weathervane remains—the one piece of the hall untouched since 1742.

In the seventeenth century, before Boston began expanding by whittling down its hills and filling in ever larger portions of the sea, this was the town dock. For decades, most of the peninsula's settlers were clustered along the then-shoreline in houses like this one, where they lived and worked. But this one, built in 1680, lasted longer than most—long enough for this and a few other photographs and lithographs to capture it before it was demolished in 1860. After their first hastily assembled thatched huts or "English wigwams" burned or tumbled down, the Puritans constructed more permanent wood houses modeled after the ones they'd left behind in Elizabethan England, with gables, overhanging stories, and roughcast (stucco) plastering. After it was occupied by merchant Thomas Standbury, who sold feather mattresses and bed ticking, this anachronistic landmark was called "the Old Feather Store."

With just a hint of its distant predecessor in the sloped design, this greenhouse was built in the 1970s as surrounding Quincy Market breathed back to life. Historian Tom O'Connor has likened Boston's successive big renewal projects in the 1960s and 1970s to a day spent cleaning the house: Once your bedroom and kitchen are spotless, you think, "Gee, now the living room looks kind of shabby." (Quincy Market being the living room.) Luckily, the city got its destructive urges out of its system before deciding to refurbish, rather than raze, the market that Mayor Josiah Quincy opened in the 1820s. The market's three long buildings are filled with shops and restaurants (such as the famous Durgin-Park, once known for its rude waitresses), the spaces in between with street performers and pushcarts. Officially Faneuil Hall Marketplace, the reuse project was the brainchild of architect Benjamin Thompson. The nearby statue of Kevin White (inset), mayor from 1968 to 1984, was unveiled in 2006.

Burlesque houses, tattoo parlors, and taverns lined the streets of the Scollay Square district, a long-established playground for sailors and slumming students by the 1950s. It had been an elegant, fashionable district in the nineteenth century (inset), as well as a hub of innovation. In his workshop there on Court Street, Thomas Edison developed his first patented invention, an electric vote-counting machine. A few years later, in the same shop, Alexander Graham Bell tested an early telephone. Nearby, actor John Wilkes Booth appeared in plays at a theater called the Boston Museum. The Sears Block (here anchored by the Court Street Tavern) was built in 1848 at the corner of Court (right) and Cornhill (left) streets, adjacent to the Sears Crescent, the 1841 building curving down Cornhill. After the turn of the century, the area's character coarsened. During the 1919 police strike, a riot—which began with a craps game and paused for a second craps game—solidified the square's rough-and-tumble reputation.

In 1963 the city hired architect I. M. Pei to devise a radical plan that swept away the twenty-two streets of Scollay Square and replaced them with a center of local, state, and federal administration. Gerhard Kallman designed the centerpiece: a stark, Brutalist city hall meant to project a break with the past for a generation reared during the Depression. The result, one critic said, "looks like the crate Faneuil Hall came in." Nevertheless, in December 1967, Mayor John Collins, nearing the end of his last term, was eager to be the first to occupy the new offices, and moved in before the building was heated. He quickly moved back out after catching pneumonia. Despite aesthetic objections, Bostonians today have grudgingly embraced Government Center, even resisting Mayor Thomas Menino's proposal to relocate the city hall to the South Boston waterfront. What remains of Scollay Square are the Sears Crescent and Block, along with the steaming kettle (above Starbucks) relocated from the demolished Oriental Tea Company.

When Scollay Square was at its boisterous peak, what one columnist termed "raffish throngs" filled theaters such as the Old Howard Athenaeum to see striptease and vaudeville acts, perhaps catching future Hollywood stars Abbott and Costello. Then they poured onto the streets to hit the bars and eateries, like Joe and Nemo's, a neighborhood institution whose hot dogs were renowned among servicemen stationed the world over. The greasy spoon was strategically situated at the corner of Cambridge and Stoddard streets, a block from the Old Howard, where between nine and eleven o'clock each night, there was "always something doing," as chronicled by David Kruh in a book of that name. While Joe and Nemo's was a popular late-night destination, it had daytime regulars as well. Here, some of them have taken a break with the employees to step outside and watch a parade, circa 1950.

Another parade is about to pass by—for the Boston Celtics, who won the 2008 NBA championship. The buildings on this side of Cambridge Street have been replaced by One, Two, and Three Center Plaza, a sweeping commercial building across from City Hall Plaza. In its lumbering fashion, Center Plaza somewhat echoes the Sears Crescent on Government Center's southern border. At approximately the site of Joe and Nemo's, instead of Stoddard Street leading up to the Old Howard (which burned down in 1961),

there's a set of steps leading to its former neighbor, the old (1893) Suffolk County Courthouse. Down the street, on the left, is King's Chapel, built in 1750, with the 1927 Parker House Hotel behind it. It's on days like this that Government Center is a lively, crowded place. And Boston has seen quite a few days like this since 2001, with three Super Bowl and two World Series celebrations, as well as the Bruins' Stanley Cup parade of 2011.

Although it was the seat of British power in the Massachusetts Bay Colony, the 1713 edifice at the head of then–King Street was paradoxically also where "the child Independence was born," as John Adams wrote. Besides the royal governor's office, it held the Massachusetts Assembly, where colonists aired grievances against the Crown. In 1770 the Boston Massacre occurred outside when redcoats fired into a hostile crowd, killing five men, including former slave Crispus Attucks. The Declaration of Independence was read from the second-floor balcony in 1776, at which point the building became the Massachusetts State House and its address changed to State Street. The state government moved to Beacon Hill in 1798, and the Old State House became a gaudy commercial building. When some suggested demolishing it to improve traffic flow at that intersection, the Bostonian Society formed in 1881 to preserve and restore the historic structure. This photo dates to 1885.

Renovation is a recurring theme at the Old State House. A subway station was built underneath it in 1903, and MBTA riders access today's Orange and Blue lines through a portal in its ancient brick exterior—which was restored to its original red in 1909. The building was damaged by a fire in 1921, then repaired. The Bostonian Society installed an HVAC system in 1992, and in 2008 they worked on restoring the wooden tower, rotted by rain over the years. As part of that project, some masonry, roof slates, and windows were replaced or repaired. Twentieth-century buildings now form a canyon around the little Old State House, which is truly dwarfed by One Beacon Street behind it. But with the Big Dig having dismantled the elevated Central Artery, ever-bustling State Street again connects with Long Wharf at its other end, and the Old State House has a clear view to the sea.

The short set of granite steps at left once led to Province House, the mansion in which the colony's royal governors lived in the 1700s. General Gage was the very last of ten officials to occupy Province House. For a short time after the British evacuated Boston, the Revolutionaries used the building as a de facto statehouse. The narrow street stretching ahead in this picture used to be a path through the gardens out behind the governor's mansion. When Province House was torn down in 1825 to make way for Rawson's Lane (later Bosworth Street), the garden was bricked over and turned into a narrow street long known as Governor's Alley. Plumbers, roofers, glazers, coal sellers, carpenters, tailors, and haberdashers made their shops on the tiny byway, seen here circa 1890. At the end of Province Street, as it was renamed, one can just make out old (1865) city hall, a French Second Empire–style building on School Street.

In the early twentieth century, Province Street was widened and the Hutchinson Building went up at right, housing an insurance company. The little granite staircase stayed intact, and a tiny barbershop opened next door to it, below street level. In 1945 the barbershop became a tavern with a legal occupancy limit of thirty-eight. The Littlest Bar, as it came to be known, was for decades a haven for downtown lawyers, construction workers, and the unemployed, while the city changed around it and skyscrapers like the Boston Company Building (1970) rose nearby. Attorney Jan Schlichtmann (played by John Travolta in the film *A Civil Action*) informally worked on cases here. The Littlest Bar closed in 2006 when its landlord, the Abbey Group, began moving forward with plans to build a thirty-one-story luxury condo tower, which is covered in scaffolding in this photograph. Protected as a historic artifact, the steps were preserved and incorporated into the design of the new tower.

Self-taught architect Charles Bulfinch's grandest contribution to Boston—and he built churches, a theater, a hotel, and a dozen private homes while serving as chief of police and head of the Board of Selectmen—was the Massachusetts State House. For the site of the Commonwealth's capitol, John Hancock donated his pasture on what was still an undeveloped Beacon Hill. Sam Adams laid the cornerstone on July 4, 1795, and the building was completed in 1797. Its Corinthian columns were of Maine pine, and its dome was shingled with whitewashed wood until 1802, when Paul Revere sheathed it in rolled copper and painted it gray. The building's redbrick walls were painted white in 1825. (Meanwhile, Bulfinch was in Washington, supervising construction of the U.S. Capitol.) In 1855 they were painted yellow. The dome was gilded in 1861. Here, the statehouse is seen shortly after its rear addition was completed in 1895.

Marble wings were added to the statehouse by 1917, and the original building's brick walls were repainted white to match them. Finally, in 1928, all the paint was removed, exposing the red brick. By tradition, on a new governor's first day in office, he gives a speech while his predecessor symbolically walks down the statehouse's long front staircase. In 1936, at the end of his lone term as governor, James Michael Curley managed to upstage his successor by leaking news beforehand that the lady he would meet at the foot of the steps had just agreed to marry him. During World War II, the dome was temporarily blackened in case of an air raid. In 1960 the pine Corinthian columns were replaced by cast iron. Around the time of this photo, a tour guide in Colonial garb remarked that the city's founding fathers would be horrified to see Bulfinch's masterpiece decorated with a giant image of a leprechaun.

Looking south from the statehouse cupola, the Boston Common is in the foreground, with Park Street on the left, intersecting Tremont Street. The oldest public green in the country, the forty-eight-acre Common began as a grazing ground for the Puritans' cows. It also held the town stocks—and the gallows, where Quaker Mary Dyer was hanged for religious dissent in 1660. (Her statue is among those on the statehouse lawn today.) Later, British troops drilled on the Common, although that didn't deter local boys from sledding down its hills as usual. (In time, the hills were carted away for landfill.) By 1905 the Common was a modern—and more peaceful—public park. Take a look at Tremont Street beyond it. Beating out even its taller next-door neighbor the twin-peaked Masonic temple, the true oddball on the block is the Greek Revival St. Paul's Cathedral, with its Ionic temple front, built in 1820.

Daniel Webster has looked out over massive war protests on the Common and to massive construction beyond. Behind the spire of Park Street Church at left, Financial District towers loom. Down the street is Tremont-on-the-Common—a balconied 1960s apartment building. Behind it is the 2001 Millennium Place. St. Paul's is still there, hidden by the growing trees of the Common, where the only major difference is unseen: an underground parking garage. The park is still a public space heavily used by Bostonians of every age and description. In the summer, thousands converge here for an annual "Hemp Fest" (officially called the "Freedom Rally") or for free Shakespeare productions. Wintertime sees families skating on the Frog Pond or attending the Christmas tree lighting ceremony. In the foreground, the 1897 relief just across Beacon Street is a memorial to Robert Gould Shaw and the Union army's first regiment of freed blacks during the Civil War.

Remnant of an earlier, failed expedition to the Shawmut peninsula, Reverend William Blackstone was Beacon Hill's sole resident when Puritans arrived from Charlestown. Even as the colonists built along the North End and the harbor, this remained a grassy series of slopes: Mount Vernon, Pemberton (or Cotton) Hill, and Sentry Hill. In 1795 painter John Singleton Copley inadvertently sold his eighteen-acre property on Mount Vernon to a building syndicate, and the area opened up to development. What may have been the nation's first gravity railroad was used to excavate sixty feet of earth from Mount Vernon's peak. It went, with the other two summits, to fill the marshes on the hill's perimeter. Charles Bulfinch built a few freestanding mansions, but with Boston's population and merchant class burgeoning rapidly, subsequent developers covered Beacon Hill (named for a never-lit tar-barrel distress signal) with three- and four-story brick row houses in the Federal, Georgian, and Victorian styles, as seen here in 1870.

After a generation as the preferred district for Boston's "Brahmins," or descendants of the original English Protestant residents, Beacon Hill went through an unfashionable phase beginning in the 1880s, when the bordering Back Bay was nearly complete. Linking the two neighborhoods, Beacon Street ran along the Mill Dam constructed over the bay before it was filled in. Soon, many were moving down the street and into the Back Bay's larger and fancier homes, to the point where some old-money families who stayed on Beacon

Hill were taking in boarders. It should be noted here that the neighborhood had never been uniformly wealthy or white; on its northern slope, toward Cambridge Street and the West End, Boston's first African American community made its home in the eighteenth century. In any event, Beacon Hill reacquired its old cachet after the 1950s. The architectural treasure trove overlooks the Common (right) across Beacon Street, now familiar to fans of TV's *Cheers* as the address of the former Bull & Finch Pub.

Well into the eighteenth century, this was a remote, unsettled neck of the woods. In fact, it was near the Neck, the narrow strip of land connecting Boston's Shawmut peninsula to the town of Roxbury on the mainland. Ropemakers eventually set up shop on this shore, but after several ropewalk fires, they wanted to sell the land as house lots. Instead, in the 1820s Mayor Josiah Quincy proposed the area be "forever after kept open . . . for the use of the citizens." Horticulturalist Horace Gray planted rare flowers here in the 1830s. Still, city councillors continued to consider selling the land. Finally, in 1856, as the city began filling in the Back Bay, the state legislature forever prohibited any construction between Beacon, Charles, Boylston, and the new Arlington Street. On this four-acre lagoon, Robert Paget artfully adapted the new bicycle technology for the first Swan Boat in 1877. In the foreground, a woman feeds some real waterfowl in 1920.

Made famous by the Mallard family in Robert McCloskey's 1941 children's book *Make Way for Ducklings*, the Public Garden is today lusher and generally more serene than its neighbor across Charles Street, the Boston Common. The twenty-four-acre public botanical garden is the first of its kind in the United States. There are close to sixty flower beds displaying tulips, pansies, and roses planted twice a year and maintained by the Boston Parks and Recreation Department. Thanks in part to the efforts of a private volunteer group, the

Friends of the Public Garden and Common, the garden holds 750 trees of 125 varieties, including a Japanese pagoda tree, a ginkgo, and twenty weeping willows around the lagoon. The Paget family still runs the Swan Boats, although they are now made of fiberglass rather than copper. In 1987 local artist Nancy Schon's bronze sculpture of the Mallard family joined the garden's more traditional statues, like the thirty-eight-foot sculpture of George Washington atop a horse at the Arlington Street entrance.

At the edge of the Common, the corner of Park Street (left) and Tremont (right) was once called "Brimstone Corner." Not so much for the sermons given at Park Street Church as for the actual brimstone, which was used to make the gunpowder that was stored in its cellar during the War of 1812. The Congregational church replaced the grain-storage barn that gave the nearby Granary Burying Ground its name. William Lloyd Garrison gave his first antislavery speech here on July 4, 1829. In an auditorium next door, Mary Baker Eddy convened the first meetings of the Christian Science Church in the 1880s. Construction began on America's first subway here in early 1895, after the city's surface trolleys (seen at right) caused more gridlock and havoc than they were worth. This photo was taken in January 1896, twenty months before the completion of the subway's first leg.

Rose-granite One Beacon Street towers over Park Street Church, while across Tremont Street, the granite, bowfront building is Suffolk University Law School. Although the fare has risen from five cents to two dollars, the station that opened in 1897 still accommodates today's Green Line, a trolley that runs aboveground on four separate branches, coming in from Jamaica Plain, Brighton, and the towns of Newton and Brookline, before descending below the streets downtown. A second story was added beneath the station in 1912 for the faster-moving train from Dorchester to Cambridge—what is now the Red Line. (The red line seen here on the sidewalk is Boston's famous Freedom Trail, a 2.5-mile path passing sixteen historical sites.) Greater Boston's train system grew, both underground and overhead, on the Boston Elevated Railway, or "BERy," network. The privately run system was turned over in 1947 to the public Metropolitan Transit Authority, which became the Massachusetts Bay Transportation Authority (MBTA) in 1964.

Elizabeth Vergoose lived here on Washington Street in the 1950s. Her second husband, printer Tom Fleet, published her nursery rhymes as *Mother Goose's Melodies for Children.* "Some," wrote George Weston, "will tell you that there is no real proof that Fleet ever published the Mother Goose book. Pay no attention to these cynics. There is no proof that he didn't." The disparately named segments of Boston's main stem coalesced as Washington Street in 1789 to honor the war-hero president upon his return visit to the city he liberated in 1776. Long the city's commercial heart, this district was consumed in the Great Fire of 1872, which destroyed sixty acres, from here to the waterfront and between Milk and Summer streets—stopping just short of the Old South Meeting House, visible at the end of the block. The city rebuilt, as evinced by this photo, taken twenty years later—while visionary German immigrant William Filene sold ready-to-wear clothing from 445–447 Washington Street.

Filene's sons moved the successful store to bigger digs in 1912. The terra-cotta building (right) was designed for them by Chicago architect Daniel Burnham. This was one of several department stores that thrived here for decades—including Jordan Marsh, Gilchrist's, Raymond's, and Kennedy's. After World War II, the pull of highways and shopping malls bode poorly for the district. Ironically, Victor Gruen, a pioneer of suburban development, helped effect the area's turnaround in the mid-1970s by designing a pedestrians-only thoroughfare and other improvements. The joint project with the MBTA and the Boston Redevelopment Authority made newly rechristened "Downtown Crossing" lively again, with all manner of people perusing its jewelry and clothing stores, and burrito and sausage stands. However, a blow to civic pride came in 2005 when Filene's closed in a national merger. Luckily, its long-separate discount spinoff, Filene's Basement, stayed open. But in 2007 it too vacated—temporarily, for an extensive renovation. Meanwhile, a thirty-nine-story multiuse development is rising next door.

Built in 1729, the Old South Meeting House had long been a survivor by the time of this 1937 photo. The building withstood an earthquake in 1744 and British occupation three decades later. It escaped the 1872 fire, and even endured a stint as a sorting room for the U.S. Post Office. The building replaced the church where Benjamin Franklin was baptized (across Milk Street from his birthplace). Before Faneuil Hall was enlarged, Old South was the alternate venue for particularly large town meetings. At one of these, in 1773, the Sons of Liberty used stage-whisper secret signals to plan the Boston Tea Party. When its congregation moved out to the New Old South Church at Copley Square in the 1870s, commercial developers eyed this vacant building's valuable land. The historic treasure was saved and turned into a museum and meeting hall by the Old South Association, an early success in the preservation movement.

The meetinghouse looks essentially the same. The Old South Association still runs the museum (with multimedia exhibits) and hosts lectures, concerts, and other events inside, and sidewalk book sales and fruit stands outside. In the foreground is part of the Boston Irish Famine Memorial. When Ireland's staple potato crop failed from 1845 to 1849, a million people died, and two million fled. About 100,000 Irish came through Boston Harbor just during the famine, and that immigration continued for decades. The Irish provided labor for the city's massive physical expansion—including filling in the Back Bay and building the transit system. Eventually, the Irish took over the town, at least politically, with many of their descendants achieving financial success as well. In 1996 developer Thomas J. Flatley, an Irish immigrant himself, chaired the committee to build a memorial to the victims of the Irish Potato Famine, and artist Robert Shure unveiled the statues and small park in 1998.

School Street (left) was the first home of Boston Latin School, the first public school in the country. Here at the corner of School and Washington streets, Anne Hutchinson lived until 1637, when she was exiled to Rhode Island for espousing such heresy as the equality of men's and women's souls. This house was built on the corner in 1712, and a succession of pharmacists lived and sold drugs here until 1828, when Timothy Carter opened the Old Corner Bookstore. (Carter also built the addition at left, along School Street.) When publishers Ticknor and Fields operated here from 1845 to 1865, the store was the hub of Boston's literary scene during its golden age. Emerson, Hawthorne, Longfellow, Thoreau, and other great American writers gathered here to socialize, and many of them wrote for the publishers' new periodical *Atlantic Monthly*. This photo, circa 1870, shows the mansard roof of the city hall peeking out over some chimneys at left.

In 1903 the owners of the Old Corner Bookstore, keeping that name, moved to a new building on Bromfield Street—not on a corner. This old building saw a variety of retailers pass through. In the 1950s, its longtime neighbors on Newspaper Row (the block to the right) began departing for bigger plants elsewhere. Bay State Camera sold projectors and film in the bookshop's old quarters, and a giant billboard hid its top two floors. In the early 1960s, the wolves circled: developers, seeing a shabby old house, envisioned a parking garage. But like its neighbor located diagonally across Washington Street (the Old South Meeting House, nearly a century earlier), this building was saved by a concerned group of citizens who raised the funds—especially from another old neighbor, the *Boston Globe*—to buy and restore it. The Globe Corner Bookstore operated here for two decades, and eventually became a jewelry store. Coincidentally, a Borders bookstore sits across School Street.

During the 1872 fire that obliterated much of what is now the Financial District, the post office was instrumental in stopping the spread of destruction. First, because the building was fireproof. Second, because the postmaster, former Civil War general William L. Burt, received the fire chief's go-ahead to use explosives to demolish buildings, thus creating a barrier to the fire. Taking the opportunity to rebuild after the conflagration, the city widened some streets and laid out Post Office Square. In 1931 the post office moved out of its former home, a French Second Empire building, and into the immense Art Deco structure seen here at center left. As automobiles became more prevalent, Bostonians parked wherever they could find room—and then other Bostonians blocked them in. Post Office Square simply turned into a big parking lot, as seen in this circa-1939 picture.

The city's first solution to the parking problem was to build a concrete parking garage here, one of many city-owned garages built in the 1950s, when Boston, like the rest of the nation, "prostrated itself before the automobile," as architectural critic Robert Campbell put it. In the late 1980s, a public-private partnership generated a better solution, one that endures as a delightful success today. The city demolished the garage, and the business group Friends of Post Office Square built a seven-level garage underground and a park above that opened in 1991. With benches and tables amid 125 varieties of trees, shrubs, and flowers, including six trees donated by the Arnold Arboretum, this gem in the middle of the Financial District is a welcome green space where lunchtime office refugees can decompress, and tourists and shoppers can rest their feet. Jane Holtz Kay posited in the *Boston Globe* that Post Office Square Park "elevated the art of city-building."

"Wharfing out," the expansion of Boston's shoreline with landfill, began in the 1630s as a series of individual projects undertaken by wharf owners. Over the decades, the process became more organized, and in 1709 the town selectmen decided to build a long wharf extending from the end of King (now State) Street, the main commercial thoroughfare, to the deep waters of the harbor, in order to accommodate large cargo ships. Two of the selectmen, Captain Oliver Noyes and Daniel Oliver, built it between 1711 and 1715.

When completed, the wharf—then called Boston Pier—was a third of a mile in length and suitably impressed traders as a grand docking point befitting North America's leading port. Lined with shops and warehouses, the wharf saw molasses (for rum), salt, leather, timber, rice, redcoats, Charles Dickens, and the region's first locomotive engine (called the *Meteor*) pass through. Europe-bound letters left here on America's first transatlantic steam route in 1840. Here the wharf thrives circa 1855.

More landfilling in the nineteenth century effectively shortened Long Wharf. Soon after the historical photo was taken, the southern "dock" (then meaning the water between wharves) was filled in to site State Street Block. As Boston slowly declined as a port, construction of Atlantic Avenue in the 1870s and then the Central Artery in the 1950s further cut the wharf, the latter demolishing most of the old warehouses save the Gardner Building (now housing the Chart House restaurant), and the 1847 granite Custom House Block (offices and apartments). Today, Long Wharf bustles not with cargo but with short-run passenger boats. The New England Aquarium runs whale watches, the MBTA runs commuter crafts to East Boston and Charlestown, and private companies run dance and rock and roll "booze cruises." This is also the point of embarkation for the Boston Harbor Islands, oft-forgotten gems now experiencing a rebirth as a recreational haven of beaches and wooded trails.

When the Boston Tea Party took place hereabouts in 1773, this was simply the southern portion of Boston Harbor. Fort Point Channel was created over the course of the nineteenth century, first as Fort Hill was dug up to extend the wharves and fill in the South Cove on the Boston side, and later as more landfill dramatically enlarged the peninsula across the way,

Dorchester Neck—or, as it was renamed after being annexed in 1804 over the objections of the ten families who lived there, South Boston. This 1963 photo shows a view from the 1874 Congress Street Bridge, with an aging, turn-of-the-century district of wavehouses and fish piers on the other side of the channel.

The Children's Museum moved from Jamaica Plain to this former wool warehouse in the late 1970s. The brick-fronted wood structure was gutted, cleaned, and reinforced with metal brackets. New windows were installed to let in the sunlight, and a glass-enclosed freight-style elevator was added to the exterior, playfully recalling the building's former purpose. At the edge of the expansive front boardwalk, a landmark snack stand has replaced the rather indifferent beverage purveyor in the old photo. The forty-foot Hood Milk Bottle was built as an ice cream stand in Taunton, Massachusetts, in 1933. H. P. Hood Company bought it from Taunton's Sankey Company in 1977 and shipped it here by barge. The other warehouses of the South Boston Waterfront, or Fort Point Historic District, are today filled with artists' lofts and architectural offices.

In the nineteenth century, five railroad companies served the South Shore, Rhode Island, and routes to New York City. Seeing the success of a union station across town on Causeway Street, these companies combined as the Boston Terminal Company to build one here at the corner of Summer Street and Atlantic Avenue. When South Station opened in 1899, it was the largest railroad terminal in the world. It also had a lower level of tracks that were never put into service. Plans for the basement included an "immigrant waiting room and lavatory." (Later, the level would house employee parking and a bowling alley.) In 1901, four years before this photo was taken, an elevated railway (just a fraction of which is visible at right) opened on Atlantic Avenue to conduct traffic between the North and South stations.

More than 700 trains used South Station on a daily basis in the early part of the century. Its busiest day ever, June 8, 1912, saw 1,001 trips on the schedule. South Station was remodeled between 1929 and 1931, closing the front entrance to automobile traffic. The Atlantic Avenue Elevated closed and was dismantled for scrap metal during World War II. Rail service declined in the 1950s, and South Station's primary occupant, the New Haven Railroad, ended all its passenger service in 1959. The Boston Redevelopment Authority (BRA) bought the building in 1965, considering the site for an office high-rise. With a rail revival in the 1970s, the BRA sold South Station to the MBTA, which today operates it with Amtrak. South Station underwent a thorough refurbishment in the 1980s, notably with the addition of eateries and shops on its impressive concourse. A bus terminal was added to the complex in 1995.

The Old Colony Railroad opened its depot (inset) in 1847. Architect G. J. F. Bryant expanded it and added the clock tower in 1867. For decades, the Old Colony ran "the boat train," a line to Fall River, from where the company's steamboats took passengers to Nantucket, Martha's Vineyard, Hyannis, "and all the Noted Seaside Resorts of Cape Cod and the South Shore of Massachusetts," as a period advertisement proclaimed. On weekdays, the last train left the depot at 5:30 p.m. This 1934 photo shows South Street stretching past the Atlantic Avenue Elevated railway toward Essex. This is the Leather District, home to tanneries and shoemakers. Once, it was all the shallow South Cove, before the railroad companies filled it in with land in the 1830s.

The Old Colony changed its name in the 1890s, then joined forces with the other railroads to build South Station, which obviated the old depot on Kneeland Street. It was torn down in 1918. There today is the Massachusetts Highway Department building (inset). A portion of South Station's bus terminal is at the left. From the opposite angle, shown in the main image, South Street hasn't changed, at least in appearance. Artists flocked to the Leather District in the 1980s, though now their lofts and galleries are giving way to offices. The diner at left has been serving frappés, hamburgers, and grilled cheese sandwiches since 1947. Long known as the Blue Diner (and as the South Street Diner since 1997), it is Boston's last classic railroad-car diner, and practically the only place for late-night grub. On weekends, after the bars close at 2:00 a.m., a mob of students, clubbers, and other nighthawks congregates cacophonously on the corner, while thirty-nine at a time dine happily inside.

Beach Street indeed ran along a shoreline, well into the nineteenth century. In 1833 a business group formed, called the South Cove Corporation, which set about filling in the tidal flats with gravel from Roxbury, creating fifty-five acres of land for terminals of the Boston and Worcester and other railroads. Tenements were completed in the 1840s, and immigrant groups cycled through. The area became largely Armenian by the turn of the century, but as early as 1869, when the transcontinental railroad was finished, some

Chinese—mostly men at first—migrated here from the West Coast and pitched tents on Ping On Alley. The small community blossomed after the Chinese Exclusion Act was repealed in 1943. By 1951, when this picture was taken, Boston's was the third-largest Chinatown in the United States, trailing only New York and San Francisco. A Yankee contemporary marveled at its drugstores stocking "sea horses, snake jelly, ground tiger bone, dried bat skins, and other horrors of the Oriental pharmacopoeia."

While the Romanesque building in the center stayed, everything else was demolished in 1954—and 300 families were displaced—to make way for the Central Artery. Over the next two decades, Chinatown felt squeezed by construction of the Massachusetts Turnpike extension on its southern border, the expansion of Tufts University–New England Medical Center to the west, and the formation of the "Combat Zone" to the north. Neighborhood activists seeking to assert Chinatown's identity got a boost in 1982 from Taiwan, which donated this impressive tile-and-marble gateway arch, raising the community's profile. For a time, Beach Street was still a through street, and trucks turning off the artery's Surface Road chipped and dented its guardian lion statues. After the Big Dig, vehicle access was blocked here and a Beijing-based firm helped design a public park suitable for lantern festivals and pickup chess games alike.

Shown here is First Christian Church, with its entrance fronting Tyler Street (left), and ground-floor storefronts facing Kneeland (right), circa 1860. Reverend Edward Edmunds led this nondenominational church for at least half a century. The New York native began preaching as an eighteen-year-old divinity student in Rhode Island in 1833, when this area was still underwater. Edmunds opened his church on Summer Street in Boston in 1843 and joined a criminal reform movement, favoring prevention over punishment. The former "costs far less," he and like-minded pastors stated in the periodical the *Prisoners' Friend* in 1848, "but human governments have yet to learn that lesson." Cofounder of a boardinghouse for young women called the Stranger's Retreat, Edmunds moved First Christian here in 1853, possibly to combat pimps who recruited rural newcomers at the railroad stations nearby. When his congregants celebrated his fiftieth year as pastor in 1893, the *New York Times* covered the occasion, reporting that Edmunds was then "the oldest settled pastor in Boston."

A seven-story loft building abuts the old row of shops and apartments down Tyler Street, the well-trod commercial and culinary artery of Chinatown. At right down Kneeland Street is the stainless-steel pagoda roof of the 1952 Chinese Merchants Association Building. The thirty-six-story One Lincoln Street Building (left of center) was completed in 2003 on the edge of Chinatown bordering the Financial District. Headquarters of the State Street Corporation, it bears a "State Street" sign similar to the one that once adorned the much less attractive 1960s State Street Bank Building (now called 225 Franklin Street). Skyscrapers like it and nearby Millennium Place represent a new downtown building boom as well as a challenge to Chinatown, which is fighting to stay affordable for immigrants—from Vietnam and Cambodia now, as well as from China—seeking a comfortable home base from which to gradually learn their adopted country's language and customs, often before moving on to Asian American communities in Dorchester, Quincy, or Brookline.

This view from circa 1908 shows the corner of Essex (left) and Washington streets. Here, 160 years prior, stood a tavern, outside which the local "South Enders" often drank under a giant elm. At times, these rough sorts ventured to the nearby Common and brawled violently with their crosstown counterparts from the North End. During an economic downturn, Samuel Adams successfully united these two factions as the formidable Sons of Liberty, and the great elm became the "Liberty Tree," an important locus of patriot activity. Effigies and coded messages hung from its branches. A Sons-led mob forced the resignation of the proposed stamp tax collector here in 1765, then celebrated the tax's repeal a year later. British troops chopped the tree down in 1775— with one of them getting killed in the process. General Lafayette later urged Bostonians to ever commemorate the spot, and the Liberty Tree Tavern opened in 1833. Its replacement, this 1850 building, features a third-floor bas-relief of the tree.

After the city razed Scollay Square in the 1960s, this district abutting Chinatown grew seedy as strip clubs, porn theaters, and prostitutes took root. In 1974 the city decided to quarantine adult entertainment by forbidding it everywhere except within a small section bordered by Washington, Essex, Kneeland, and Harrison. The "Combat Zone" flourished throughout the 1970s and into the 1980s. Exercising perhaps not the kind of liberty the Sons had in mind, the storefront directly under the tree-site marker declared "Movies—Nude Photos." Constant opposition from the neighboring Chinese community and Tufts–New England Medical Center, along with the advent of VCRs, doomed the Combat Zone. Two strip clubs remain on LaGrange Street (which is named, incidentally, for the aforementioned Lafayette's summer estate). Today, this building houses the Massachusetts Registry of Motor Vehicles.

More than 735 acres of tidal flats once lay between peninsular Boston and mainland Roxbury. Copley Square was one of the last portions of land made—with sand, gravel, and even trash shipped by rail from Needham— in what is today called the Back Bay. The distinctive Trinity Church was designed by the New Orleans–raised, Paris-schooled architect Henry Hobson Richardson and built between 1872 and 1877 on top of two thousand wooden piles and four giant granite slabs. Public buildings across the country imitated the lively Richardson Romanesque style for the rest of the century. When the Hotel Westminster (right) was completed in 1903, it exceeded the neighborhood's ninety-foot height limit. After a series of suits and countersuits, the U.S. Supreme Court ruled that the hotel had to lop off its top six feet. Work on that is seen in this circa-1905 picture.

April 15, 2013, began like every Patriots' Day in Massachusetts. Hundreds of thousands of people lined the route of the Boston Marathon, from Hopkinton in the west to a spot just shy of Copley Square. More than 26,000 runners from the world over competed. By 2:49 p.m., the leaders were long done; those crossing the finish line now were achieving personal triumphs or raising money for charity, cheered on by their friends and relatives. That's when two homemade bombs went off, killing three people and injuring 264—maiming some for life. The two suspected bombers shot a police officer in the back four days later, before one was killed and the other captured. Someday, a permanent memorial to the victims will likely be erected here or nearby. For now, a makeshift memorial attracts personal artifacts and tributes, expressions of sadness, solidarity, and resilience.

The first John Hancock Tower—the pyramid-topped edifice peeking over the church's shoulder here—was built in 1949. After its rival insurance company, Prudential, built a taller skyscraper nearby, Hancock responded with a new, sixty-story tower—ironically, on the former site of the carefully pruned Hotel Westminster. Designed by I. M. Pei and Partners and built from 1968 to 1976, the skinny giant strangely deflects attention by reflecting the sky, and is widely considered a decent-looking skyscraper compared to the downtown flattops of that area. The tower rests on a concrete mat supported by piles driven through the landfill and into the bedrock, 160 feet below sea level. Engineers had to reinforce the building's steel and replace its windows after a storm early on, and on the fifty-eighth floor, according to the American Institute of Architects' *Guide to Boston*, a "rolling weight on a film of oil" allows the building to shift against high winds.

Any case for the validity of Boston's "Athens of America" moniker has to include the fact that it was the nation's first big city to open a public library. (It also opened the first branch library, in East Boston.) Prior to the 1850s, the private Boston Athenaeum had a monopoly on book lending, but even some of its own trustees felt a free library would make a desirable addition to the growing city—in part to help assimilate new immigrants who, it was presumed, knew little of the "native" culture or literary tradition. From earlier cramped quarters, the Boston Public Library moved down Boylston Street to its present location on Copley Square in 1895. Designed by Charles McKim, the Italian Renaissance Revival "people's palace" of Milford granite took eight years to build soundly on the fresh land of the Back Bay. This photo was taken shortly after the library opened.

At far right is the library's workaday 1972 addition, designed by Philip Johnson. It was built of granite and to the same scale as the ornate McKim building, although it looks radically different otherwise. Inside, it isn't especially easy to get from one building to the other. But taken together, the tandem holds at least seven million volumes, or a million pounds of books, plus hundreds of thousands of maps and government documents. Everybody from sixth-graders to grad students to published scholars come to the Boston Public Library to research one topic or another. The library includes extensive photo archives and a comprehensive local reference shelf. Besides the obvious development of towers and hotels along Boylston Street, trolleys haven't run aboveground at Copley since the 1960s. Below the surface, the Green Line station here is undergoing a renovation that is, speaking of library books, long overdue.

Built in 1901 on a former circus lot, Huntington Avenue Grounds hosted the game of baseball's first World Series. The American League's Boston Americans went on to beat the National League's Pittsburgh Pirates, five games to three. Here, Cy Young threw the modern era's first perfect game for Boston in 1904. Renamed the Red Sox in 1907, the team was a favorite of working-class Bostonians who now had some disposable income, typified by the Irish-Americans who largely made up the Royal Rooters, an early fan club. Men would walk here from nearby Roxbury or ride the trolley (foreground) from other neighborhoods to watch the local nine play teams like the Detroit Tigers, as in this 1911 photo. Obviously, the stadium's seating capacity of 9,000 was insufficient, as its ludicrously deep center field (635 feet) was shortened by spectators. The bordering rail yard belongs to the New York, New Haven, and Hartford Railroad. Beyond that lies the South End.

The Red Sox moved across the Fens to Fenway Park the season after the historical photo was taken. Northeastern University moved to the neighborhood in 1913, and built the Cabot Physical Education Center on the old Huntington Avenue Grounds site in 1955. A statue of Cy Young (inset) was unveiled in 1993 in a nearby courtyard, about where the pitcher's mound had been. The Cabot is the third building from the bottom in the main photo, taken from Northeastern's new high-rise residence hall. Long a commuter college, Northeastern has seen explosive growth recently, with ten new dorms since 1995. The campus takes up both sides of Huntington Avenue seen here. Past where the trolley goes underground and the avenue curves left, the long, low brick building at left is Symphony Hall, near the dome of the Christian Science complex. Between the Prudential and Hancock skyscrapers is 111 Huntington Avenue, which was built in 2002 and nicknamed "the R2D2 Building" for its rounded top.

After the Back Bay was filled in, 170 acres of tidal flats still lay to its west. Sewage drained into it from Brookline via the Muddy River and from Roxbury via Stony Brook, so that at low tide the area stunk to high heaven. Landscape architect Frederick Law Olmsted devised the solution in 1880. The two small rivers were diverted into the Charles through covered conduits; the basin was dredged, and a dam kept it covered in salt water. A winding waterway took shape through dumped gravel under a layer of topsoil planted with vegetation. To the banks of the Back Bay Fens, as Olmsted named his creation, came the Museum of Fine Arts in 1909, after just three decades in its previous location on Copley Square. The neoclassical granite building is seen here shortly after its Fens-facing Evans Wing opened in 1915. (The museum fronts Huntington Avenue.) In the distance at right is Roxbury's Mission Church.

Shot from the Fenway, the road running alongside this portion of the Fens, the museum is here days away from a reopening ceremony for its north entrance, locked since the 1970s. For the past three decades, most visitors have entered through I. M. Pei's West Wing addition on their way to see Greek vases, Nubian fertility masks, or the largest collection of Claude Monet paintings outside France. With the Evans Wing reopening, the museum is working to reestablish the north-south axis that its architect, Guy Lowell, envisioned. The Huntington Avenue entrance was renovated in 2009. The Fens entrance now features expanded stairs and a wheelchair ramp, as well as the fountains seen at left and right. A new East Wing, which houses American art, opened in 2010. As for the (now freshwater) Fens, it is lined on sunny days with people playing softball, bicycling, walking, and tending community gardens.

After the death of her husband Jack—heir to the fortune of a merchant prince of Boston's India trade—Isabella Stewart Gardner began building a home big enough for all the art the couple had collected during extensive world travel: 2,500 objects in all, encompassing textiles, sculptures, furniture, silver, rare books—and paintings, including Titian's *Rape of Europa* and Rembrandt's *Self-Portrait*. The "Whim of a Woman," scoffed one headline writer as Gardner supervised construction of an Italian Renaissance–styled palace on the Fens.

Raising Boston's eyebrows never bothered the flamboyant New York native. Historian Susan Wilson debunks some of the taller tales, though: Gardner escorted an old lion around a zoo once; she didn't walk pet lion cubs down Tremont Street. Nor did she likely have flings with her admittedly many male friends. "She did, however," writes Wilson, "attend a concert at Symphony Hall wearing a headband that read, 'Oh, You Red Sox.' " This picture was snapped not long after Gardner took residence in 1902.

Gardner regularly opened her home to the public before her death in 1924. In her will, she left it to the city as a museum, stipulating that nothing in it be moved or rearranged. The result is a charmingly chaotic sort of "anti-museum," with tapestries draped over antique chairs, and paintings from a jumble of eras and countries cluttering the walls. Of course, curatorial staff clean and restore works and allow research, and a 1932 addition exhibits traveling collections. In a shocking 1990 heist, two thieves impersonating policemen entered the museum, bound the guards, and made off with Vermeer's *The Concert*, a rare Rembrandt, and ten other works. Valued at $200 million, the paintings have never resurfaced. While a blow, the robbery hasn't diminished the Gardner's appeal. The eclectic collection still fascinates, and the museum continues to host classical concerts and other programs. And its beautiful, glass-roofed inner courtyard, planted seasonally with orchids and tumbling nasturtiums, is truly one of Boston's treasures.

The filled-in land around Frederick Law Olmsted's Back Bay Fens was Boston's new frontier at the turn of the twentieth century. Where once lay a no-man's-land of tidal flats plus the mainland marshes of Roxbury's Gravelly Point, streets were now laid out, and cultural institutions took root. These include the Museum of Fine Arts and the Gardner Museum, as well as the Massachusetts Historical Society, Symphony Hall, the New England Conservatory of Music, Simmons College, and Harvard Medical School— all built between 1899 and 1909. Boston Latin School and hospitals including Children's and Boston Lying-In were built near the Fenway, and a residential neighborhood sprouted between the Fens and Boylston Street. This picture was taken in 1909, looking down Lansdowne Street from Brookline Avenue. The dome of the Christian Science World Headquarters on Massachusetts Avenue is on the horizon at right. The church moved there from Park Street in 1893, and built the Classical Revival basilica by 1906.

Home of the Boston Red Sox, Fenway Park (right) was built in 1912 and renovated after a major fire in 1934. It is difficult to overstate the place Fenway Park—oldest and smallest park in the major leagues—holds in the hearts of New Englanders. The Sox won five World Series before trading power-hitting pitcher Babe Ruth to the New York Yankees, and entering an eighty-six-year title drought that ended in 2004, literally as a blue moon occurred in the night sky. Fenway's most famous feature is its thirty-seven-foot left-field wall, the "Green Monster." Behind it, seats (seen here hanging over Lansdowne Street) were added in 2003. Straight ahead, the fifty-two-story Prudential Tower (1965) is Boston's Eiffel Tower, seemingly visible from anywhere in eastern Massachusetts. The left side of Lansdowne is lined with bars and nightclubs. A prime pre- and post-game watering hole, the Cask'n Flagon recently underwent a facelift. It has been recognized as one of the top sports bars in the United States.

This was originally Sewall's Point, on the marshy shore of the town of Brookline. Seen here in 1910, Governor's Square, as it was then called, was the confluence of two major boulevards created in nineteenth-century land-making projects. From the upper left-hand corner of the photo to the lower right runs Beacon Street, once a roadway atop the Mill Dam spanning the waters of the Back Bay. From lower left, through the square, and off into the center distance runs Commonwealth Avenue, the leafy spine of the new Back Bay, a fashionable neighborhood developed on the infill land a few decades prior. When Boston annexed Brighton in 1874, Brookline graciously ceded Sewall's Point and a strip of land along the Charles River so that Brighton could connect to the central city via Commonwealth Avenue. (Aside from that gesture, Brookline was ever to remain a town separate from Boston.) Several elegant hotels opened on the square, including the Hotel Buckminster, seen here at right.

The Red Sox moved to nearby Fenway Park two years after the historical photo was taken, making the square's trolley stop (subsequently moved underground) busier than ever. One of baseball's biggest scandals was born in the Hotel Buckminster when a bookie met there with a Chicago White Sox player to plot the throwing of the 1919 World Series. A year later, the square was officially renamed after the Kenmore Hotel. The landmark electric Citgo sign was erected in 1965. Kenmore Square was long home to the famous punk rock dive bar the Rathskeller, or "the Rat." It closed in 1997; most of that block was demolished for today's Hotel Commonwealth. Runners of the Boston Marathon, the world's oldest annual marathon, have passed through Kenmore Square every Patriots' Day since 1897. Tragically, the 2013 marathon was halted after two bombs exploded near the finish line, preventing many participants from finishing the race.

A few trolley stops up Commonwealth Avenue from Kenmore Square, this was the home of the Braves, Boston's National League team, from 1915 through 1952, when this photo was taken. Note the sparse crowds—and that was opening day. The Braves had enjoyed periods of popularity, drawing half a million fans in 1933. Even just four years prior to this photo, the Braves were in the World Series; they lost to the Cleveland Indians in what could be considered a battle of the politically incorrect team names. They played the longest game in baseball history here on May 1, 1920, a twenty-six-inning 1–1 tie with the Brooklyn Dodgers. Babe Ruth returned to Boston to play his final games as a Brave in 1935. The team moved to Milwaukee in 1953.

Boston University purchased the field months after the historic photo was taken, although that didn't mean the end of professional sports on what is now Nickerson Field. The Boston Patriots, forerunner of today's New England Patriots of the National Football League, played here from 1960 to 1962. This picture was taken the morning of Boston University's 2008 graduation ceremony; two hours later, Boston Red Sox president Larry Lucchino gave the commencement address on the site of the Braves' former home. Beyond the stadium, the National Guard Armory has been replaced with the Agganis Arena and the residential towers of the new Student Village, or "StuVi." One of the largest institutions in town, Boston University boasts some distinguished alumni, including Martin Luther King Jr. and actress Geena Davis.

Without significant waterways like those linking their rival port of New York City to the interior, Bostonians moved quickly to establish a railroad running west, via Worcester, in the 1830s. Lines were built along the Charles River and through Allston, a section of the town of Brighton known for its stockyards and slaughterhouses. The move was key to keeping Boston economically relevant. Built in 1886 for the Boston and Albany Railroad, the Allston Depot was designed by Shepley, Rutan, and Coolidge, successor firm to H. H. Richardson's. While this site was obviously associated with steam-powered freight and passenger trains, it was also the departure point for Boston's first electric-powered streetcar, which emerged from a barn behind the depot and traveled up Harvard Street (barely visible at the street corner, at far left) to Coolidge Corner in Brookline. This photo is from 1900.

Designated a historic landmark, the building is today familiar to commuters on the Massachusetts Turnpike. It has housed the Sports Depot, a sports bar and restaurant, since 1988 (excluding a dark period when management briefly transformed it into a seafood restaurant called Captain Fishbone's). With dozens of flat-screen televisions, the bar is always packed with die-hard fans of all sports. At the far left, the Allston Block stands empty, but a local artist has decorated its windows with images of neighborhood figures (inset), such as the late Mr. Butch, a widely beloved street musician, shown here holding his trademark suitcase. Butch died in a scooter accident on Cambridge Street by the depot. Allston today is undeniably shabby in parts, but it works for a unique community of students, recent grads, hipsters, and Brazilian immigrants.

This photo shows the intersection of Washington and Market streets in Brighton, circa 1910. Previously, Brighton was a farming town, and this was the crossroads of the region's livestock trade. The white, wooden Greek Revival building on the far corner at right was built in 1818 as Agricultural Hall, site of a prominent state fair and cattle show every October for twenty years. Brighton once had around fifty slaughterhouses, but greater public health awareness and new refrigerated railroad cars reduced that to one big abattoir on the Charles. Speculators began buying up the area's farms to divide and sell as house lots, and by 1874, Brighton had transformed from a rural village into a residential neighborhood of Boston, with paved streets, sidewalks, and modern sewers. Electric streetcars were introduced in the 1880s, quickening development. At left, the four-story building with the domed corner oriel is the new Imperial Hotel and Washington Building. Dennis Rourke opened the drugstore on the first floor in 1905.

Rourke's Pharmacy became a neighborhood institution where, for ninety years, people bought things like cough syrup, cameras, and razors while their kids got ice cream at the soda fountain. Denny Rourke's son and daughters ran the shop until the last of them, Mary, died in 1997. In their wills, the siblings left large sums to Boston College and the Sisters of St. Joseph, two of several Catholic institutions that migrated here from the South End in the twentieth century, giving Brighton the nickname "Little Rome." Another is

St. Elizabeth's Hospital, seen here in the distance, at center. Founded by laywomen of the Third Order of St. Francis, the hospital moved here in 1914 and rebuilt entirely in 1992. Agricultural Hall is still at right; the oldest building in Brighton Center, it houses the local branch of Main Streets, Boston's neighborhood revitalization program. No streetcar has rattled this way since 1968, when the MBTA discontinued the A line. The tracks weren't removed until 1998.

In the 1770s, Boston was still just a tiny peninsula. Down the coast to Boston's south lay the much larger (in area) town of Dorchester. Jutting into the harbor from mainland Dorchester was another peninsula, called Dorchester Neck. On the neck were a pair of hills—Dorchester Heights. It was on these heights that General George Washington and his Continental troops placed cannons in March 1776, forcing the British redcoats occupying Boston to evacuate. Later, in 1804, Boston annexed Dorchester Neck, renaming it South Boston. In 1902, after the heights' eastern summit had long since been excavated for fill, Evacuation Monument (seen in the main image from 1909) was built on extant Telegraph Hill. Looking toward Boston from the hill in 1855 (above), one can just make out the Massachusetts State House dome on the horizon at center. On the water at right, the Boston, Hartford and Erie Railroad curves out over the South Boston Flats.

The 137-foot white marble Evacuation Monument is unchanged, unlike the neighborhood around it and the city below. South Boston became predominantly Irish by World War I, though it also had considerable pockets of Polish and Lithuanian immigrants. "Southie" retains a blue-collar Irish-American community today, but it has also seen an influx of young professionals—some of whom are Boston College grads of Irish descent, returning to the city of their grandparents. Just as Charlestown has its obelisk and parade to mark a turning point in pre-Revolution hostilities, Southie holds a (better-known) parade that passes its (lesser-known) monument on "Evacuation Day"—which, serendipitously, is also St. Patrick's Day. Looking toward Boston from Dorchester Heights today, the water where the railroad ran has been gradually filled in and extensively developed. The giant white hangarlike structure is the new Boston Convention and Exhibition Center. To its left are the brick warehouses of the old South Boston Waterfront. In the distance are Rowe's Wharf and I. M. Pei's Harbor Towers.

Southie residents sun and swim on Pleasure Bay, at City Point, in 1930. Created just a few years prior, the beach and causeway connect the mainland with once-separate Castle Island (just off camera at right). The "castle" is Fort Independence, built in the 1850s, the latest of several fortifications on the island going back to 1634. In 1827 Boston native Edgar Allan Poe was stationed there, and fellow artillerymen told him a Castle Island legend that inspired his short story "The Cask of Amontillado." At left is the dry dock added to South Boston's waterfront around the turn of the century to accommodate larger vessels. A thousand acres of land—more than the Back Bay—were added to South Boston in the nineteenth and twentieth centuries, mostly for industrial use. Decades after Frederick Law Olmsted envisioned a public park with a curved shoreline here, a series of federal and state dredging and landfilling projects finally realized his plan by the 1920s.

It's spring, a little early for a dip in New England waters. Not that the cold bothers everybody; at neighboring L Street Beach, Southie's famous L Street Brownies take an invigorating plunge every New Year's Day. Indeed, between South Boston, Dorchester, and East Boston, the city is blessed with several public beaches along Boston Harbor, a once heavily polluted body that underwent an amazing $4 billion cleanup in the 1990s. Enclosed by a dike since the 1950s, Pleasure Bay is still the cleanest of the beaches.

Visible across the bay, Fort Independence has been a museum since the U.S. military decommissioned it in 1962. Castle Island and Pleasure Bay, with the beach, walkways, playground, fishing pier, and, of course, Sullivan's takeout joint, which has sold hot dogs and fried clams since 1951, is a local favorite weekend afternoon getaway. The nearby dry dock is still one of the largest on the East Coast; the RMS *Queen Elizabeth 2* was repaired there in 1992.

The traditional boundary between South Boston and Dorchester, Andrew Square is being torn up in 1916 during work on a subway extension. The Cambridge Subway, opened in 1912 between Harvard Square and Park Street, had proven a big success, and southern commuters clamored for rapid-transit access. The Dorchester Tunnel connected Park Street to Andrew Square, once known as Washington Village. It was an expensive and disruptive project, requiring trolleys to be diverted and entire three-story houses to be moved. This view is from the end of Southampton Street (a route over the newly filled South Bay), looking across Dorchester Avenue, previously known as Federal Street or the Dorchester Turnpike. Also branching from this intersection are Dorchester Street, Preble Street, and Boston Street.

The Andrew Square project was such an ordeal that when officials wanted to extend the route to Ashmont in 1924, they decided to use existing tracks of the New Haven Railroad rather than build another subway. Known as the Red Line today, and since extended north into Somerville and south into Braintree and Quincy, the route is still the MBTA's most heavily traveled. With the trains rumbling safely underground, Andrew Square's surface looks a little more placid right now. But at peak driving times, this is one of the most harrowing intersections in Boston. Stretching five miles from South Station to Lower Mills, Dorchester Avenue, or "Dot Ave," is slated for improvements, and this hub may soon benefit from lane closings, pedestrian plazas, trees, and other traffic-calming measures.

Not to be confused with South Boston (or with the South End of eighteenth-century peninsular Boston), the South End was created in the 1830s and 1840s when the city filled in the tidal flats on either side of the Neck, the oft-flooded isthmus that barely connected Boston to the mainland at Roxbury. Extended from downtown, Tremont Street was one of the first streets laid out on the new land. The Cyclorama was built here in 1884. Inside was a 50-by-400-foot panoramic painting of the battle of Gettysburg. Artist Paul

Philippoteaux achieved an astonishing realism based on countless source photos and interviews with survivors. He placed shoes, flags, and cannons between the painting and the spectators' walk for a three-dimensional effect. Civil War veterans who viewed it cried. Here, a line forms, possibly on July 4, 1885. Behind the Cyclorama are the neighborhood's bowfronted row houses, and on the horizon at left, the campanile of the Back Bay's New Old South Church.

Philippoteaux's painting was a smashing success, even spawning an imitator two blocks down Tremont Street that depicted the battle of Bunker Hill. After five years, the Cyclorama closed the Gettysburg painting and exhibited a new panorama, of the battle of Little Big Horn, or "Custer's Last Stand." In 1890 the building was purchased by John Gardner. It hosted athletic contests, including bicycle races and a boxing match featuring Roxbury's John L.

Sullivan, the last bare-knuckle champion. In 1922 the Cyclorama's medieval-style entrance was remodeled, and the original tin roof was replaced by a glass dome 127 feet in diameter. The altered building today houses the Boston Center for the Arts, a nonprofit organization that provides studio, theater, and gallery space for local visual and performing artists.

Most locals can tell you that Boston Latin School, the country's oldest public school (founded in 1635, a year before Harvard), was once located on School Street downtown, and that today it sits on Avenue Louis Pasteur in the Fenway. Less remembered is that for forty-one years, Latin School shared a mammoth building with its rival, Boston English High School, on Montgomery Street in the South End, seen here in 1888. Alma mater of John Hancock, Charles Bulfinch, and Wendell Phillips, the prestigious

Boston Latin School had lately been turning out a scrappy new breed of alumni—men like John F. "Honey Fitz" Fitzgerald, a Boston mayor and John F. Kennedy's grandfather. Around World War I, John Marquand's fictional old-monied Bostonian George Apley discovered that a crooked lawyer named O'Reilly "went to the Boston Latin School, which proves that I was right in always thinking that this school has been losing its grip since my father's time."

Boston Latin School moved to its present location between Simmons College and Brigham and Women's Hospital in 1922. Boston English followed, for a time sitting right across Louis Pasteur from Latin. In the years since, Nation of Islam leader Louis Farrakhan (who transferred to English) and Michael Patrick MacDonald, author of *All Souls: A Family Story from Southie*, have joined Benjamin Franklin among the ranks of well-known Latin dropouts. Twentieth-century graduates include composer Leonard Bernstein, conductor Arthur Fiedler, and Rob Lind (a.k.a. "White Trash Rob") and Erick Medina (a.k.a. "Buddha") of the hard-core punk band Blood for Blood, as well as actress Christine Elise (*Beverly Hills 90210*). As for this space on Montgomery Street today, it is the parking lot behind another structure built for two schools: McKinley Elementary and Boston Technical High School, the latter being, coincidentally, an exam school, like Latin. Tech moved to Roxbury and became the John D. O'Bryant School in 1991.

With Boston's Irish population booming in the mid-nineteenth century, the Roman Catholic Archdiocese of Boston felt that its Charles Bulfinch–designed cathedral downtown on Franklin Street was metaphorically bursting at the seams. Seeking room for an expansive structure more appropriate for its numbers, the archdiocese looked to the up-and-coming South End. Using Roxbury puddingstone, Patrick Keeley built the imposing Cathedral of the Holy Cross on Washington Street between 1867 and 1875. When completed, it was 120 feet high and 364 feet long, with pews accommodating 3,500 parishioners. The largest Catholic church in the United States at that time, the cathedral rivaled London's Westminster Abbey for size. The cardinal lived in a mansion on the premises. In 1901 the Boston Elevated Railway opened its line down Washington Street, blighting the cathedral site (above).

The neighborhood around the cathedral turned shabby quickly, and Cardinal William Henry O'Connell decided to move out west. In 1918, after a stint in the Back Bay, O'Connell built a mansion, offices, and seminary in the rolling green hills of Brighton with money bequeathed by theater owner Benjamin F. Keith. (In 2004 the archdiocese sold that land to the Jesuits across Commonwealth Avenue at Boston College, and moved operations to an office park in Braintree by 2008.) However, Boston's cardinals have continued to serve Mass here at Holy Cross every Sunday. In 1987 the MBTA dismantled the Elevated Railway and realigned its Orange Line (named for Washington Street's former colonial identity as Orange Street) as part of the Southwest Corridor project. Today, the train runs along a canyon set below street level.

This is the intersection of two of Boston's longest and most storied roads. So named in 1789, Washington Street, to the right, was the sole route along the Neck linking Boston to the mainland in the seventeenth and eighteenth centuries. (Reflecting the reverence accorded the founding father, there are in fact six streets named Washington within city limits, and thirty-six in the metropolitan area.) At left, Massachusetts Avenue would eventually run from Dorchester to Arlington, eight miles distant, crossing a river and passing two university behemoths on the way. In this 1860s photo, however, it is merely West Chester Park, a side street of the South End. At this time, the briefly fashionable neighborhood of ornate brick and brownstone row houses, hardly a generation old, is about to get some competition from its better-looking younger sister, the Back Bay.

By the turn of the century, West Chester extended across both filled-in districts, the South End and Back Bay. Almost as soon as well-to-do young Boston families had another residential option—one closer to Beacon Hill and offering views of the Charles—they abandoned the South End, and their town houses and mansions became tenements and rooming houses for struggling Irish, Greek, Lebanese, and Syrian immigrants. A large African American population took root here, and jazz clubs dotted the area in the

1940s. One, Wally's Café, is still on Massachusetts Avenue a few blocks away. Moderate gentrification began in the 1970s, and the diverse neighborhood today features art galleries, gay bars, upscale restaurants, and a radical-leftist book store, as well as the Boston Medical Center. In order to open a 7-Eleven in this historic district, the corporation had to agree to use muted hues on a tasteful exterior.

Dudley Square is actually a triangle, the intersection of the present Washington, Warren, and Dudley streets—all rural transportation routes laid out deliberately in the seventeenth century. The Puritans who in 1630 settled this region of rocky hills organized in 1652 as the township of Roxbury, encompassing a swath of land that includes today's neighborhoods of Mission Hill, Jamaica Plain, Roslindale, and West Roxbury. Drawn by its ample fields, timber, and water (from Stony Brook), Roxbury's people chiefly made their living from the earth. For two centuries, their orchards produced Roxbury russet apples, a key ingredient in cider, long a staple beverage locally. Growing in population, Roxbury incorporated as a city in 1846. Here, self-conscious residents pose for a photograph at the corner of Dudley Street (left) and Warren Street (right) in 1860.

In 1867 the residents of Roxbury voted, by a three-to-one margin, for annexation to Boston—partly to solve water and sewer problems and also to ensure street improvements. Several towns followed suit, boosting Boston's population by 200,000 in ten years. Dudley Square grew in prominence, and the grand Hotel Dartmouth was built in 1871. This marble-faced French Second Empire edifice, with seven Queen Anne–style towers, was a residential hotel for successful Roxbury merchants who enjoyed easy access to Boston via first the streetcar, then the Elevated Railway, after it was completed in 1899. In 1910 a train infamously derailed and crashed onto Dudley Street, killing the driver. Over time, the Dartmouth turned into a rooming house, then closed altogether, its upper floors boarded up for thirty years. In 2002 a nonprofit community development group bought and refurbished the building, reopening it for housing.

William Shirley was a royal governor of the Massachusetts Bay Colony, reporting directly to King George II and at one point serving as commander-in-chief of all the British armed forces in North America. He built this regal residence in rural Roxbury between 1747 and 1751. Scholars believe Shirley commissioned Peter Harrison to design the Georgian country house; Harrison would soon gain renown as the architect of King's Chapel in Boston and, later, the Vassall-Craigie-Longfellow House, the 1759 mansion in Cambridge where Henry Wadsworth Longfellow would live for most of his life. After the former colonies won independence, another governor lived here—this time an American, William Eustis, a Revolutionary War surgeon who served as governor of the young commonwealth of Massachusetts in the 1820s. His much younger wife lived here until her death in 1865; her distant relatives inherited the house (shown here circa 1867) and divided it for apartments.

The mansion's surroundings changed drastically in the last third of the nineteenth century. Streets were laid out around its relatively small grounds, and builders lined them with small one- and two-unit houses for the working- and middle-class families moving out of Boston's central districts in search of green space and fresh air. Roxbury was destined to become primarily Irish and Jewish by 1920, and primarily black by 1970. In 1913, fresh off founding the Society for the Preservation of New England Antiquities, William Sumner

Appleton, concerned for the fate of this now-abandoned architectural artifact, started the Shirley-Eustis House Association to purchase and care for it. In the late 1960s, when vandalism and fires plagued its urban neighborhood, the association resisted pressure to move the house, and it remains in place and intact today, one of only four Colonial-era governor's mansions left in the country.

Malcolm X (born Malcolm Little) lived here on Dale Street as a teenager with his sister, Ella Little-Collins, during World War II. In his autobiography, Malcolm X described a stratified Roxbury of native "Black Brahmins," Southern transplants, and Jamaicans. Exploring Boston, he discovered "one statue in the Boston Common [that] astonished me: a Negro named Crispus Attucks, [the] first man to fall in the Boston Massacre." The Parker House busboy was drawn to Roxbury's ghetto and "the sharp-dressed young 'cats' who hung on the corners and in the poolrooms" and sported "conked" hair. Turning to crime, Little was soon convicted of burglary and served seven years in the state prison in Charlestown, where he read voraciously and studied Nation of Islam leader Elijah Muhammad's teachings and changed his surname to X. Paroled in 1952, Malcolm X led Temple Eleven in Roxbury—with a young Louis Farrakhan as understudy—until 1957, when he went on to Harlem and a larger role in the movement. After moderating his rhetoric, Malcolm X was assassinated in 1965.

In the late 1960s, many middle-class blacks and whites fled Roxbury as crime rose sharply; the flight accelerated when arsonists began torching the vacated buildings. Ella Little-Collins abandoned her house in the 1970s, and it stayed empty throughout the 1980s. From its lowest point about 1990, the neighborhood rebounded thanks to a combination of concerted city efforts, church initiatives, improved police-community relations, and a general backlash against gangs. Ella died in 1996, but the Little-Collins family returned to Roxbury and restored her old property. In 1998 the private home officially received landmark status, exemplifying how "the city's racial and ethnic diversity is increasingly recognized in historical writing and preservation efforts," notes historian Lawrence Kennedy. The designation of an "ordinary-looking Roxbury house [as] a historical landmark by the Boston Landmarks Commission is remarkable" and evinces "a more inclusive understanding of the past."

In 1871, as the city built Huntington Avenue (center) out to newly annexed Roxbury, the Redemptorist Brothers opened Our Lady of Perpetual Help on Tremont Street (left) at the foot of Roxbury's Parker Hill, one marshy mile from the edge of the South End. Mission Church, as it came to be known, anchored the settlement of Irish who came here to work in the puddingstone quarry or the breweries on the back of the hill. The Parker family's apple orchards soon gave way to streets lined with Queen Anne–style houses, and

Mission Church parishioners started to refer to their neighborhood as Mission Hill. The horsecar line here was electrified in the 1890s, assuring Huntington Avenue's development as an urban corridor. By the 1940s, automobiles overran Boston's streets, but the trolleys continued to ferry commuters and shoppers between Park Street and bustling Mission Hill, and this intersection of Huntington Avenue and Tremont, Calumet (center left), and Francis (right) streets could be daunting.

Today, the trolley stop has better curbing, signage, and an all-around heftier and safer presence thanks to overhauls in the 1980s and 2000s. Consequently, Huntington Avenue has been narrowed, a traffic-calming measure compounded by brightly painted crosswalks. However, this still isn't the world's easiest intersection to navigate. The neighborhood around it has changed, at least demographically, with a black community emerging in the 1960s. Disco diva Donna Summer grew up in Mission Hill, and later R&B star Bobby Brown was raised in the Mission Main housing project, behind the church. Notoriously, suburbanite Charles Stuart shot and killed his wife on Francis Street in 1989, blaming it on "a black guy" and briefly setting back race relations. Mission Hill is very diverse today, with Latinos, blacks, Irish-Americans, and newer "off-the-boat" Ireland natives. It is also home to doctors and nurses who work in the bordering Longwood Medical Area, and to students from nearby colleges like Northeastern University.

Jamaica Plain was once part of bucolic West Roxbury, which was a distinct town merely from 1851, when it split from Roxbury, until 1874, when it merged with Boston. The district's main thoroughfare, Centre Street, is seen here circa 1895. Second from left is a fire station, with the spire of the First Baptist Church rising beyond. Note the trolley in the distance: along with improved water delivery and sanitary engineering, the development of a transit system (however initially disorganized) propelled Boston's expansion southwestward into the "streetcar suburbs." Middle-class men could keep their jobs downtown while attempting to live out the rural ideal with their families in detached wood-frame homes in the hinterlands. A railway for horse-drawn cars was laid out along Centre Street in the late 1850s, and electrified in the early 1890s. Industry came to Jamaica Plain when brewers built along its Stony Brook, leading to yet more residential construction as the German and Irish immigrants who worked in the breweries settled nearby.

After several temporary stoppages in the 1970s and 1980s, the MBTA closed the Arborway trolley line for major repairs in 1985. Track was relaid and service resumed along Huntington Avenue from Symphony Hall, through Brigham Circle, and to Heath Street in Jamaica Plain. However, service was never restored on Centre Street. The tracks were paved over in 2000. The modified old fire station is now the headquarters of J. P. Licks, one of the best-known ice cream sellers in a region historically full of them—from the classic Bailey's and Brigham's to the modern Toscanini's and Emack & Bolio's. Jamaica Plain today is a lively, diverse neighborhood with Hispanic families, Irish old-timers, and a strong community of "socialists, communists, lesbians, liberal progressives, Cambridge-type intellectuals, yuppies, [and] hippies," as the *Boston City Paper* describes it.

Former summer home of the Mattapan Wampanoags, this kettle of glacial meltwater in the wilds of then–West Roxbury provided Boston with most of its water, via a system of wooden pipes, from 1795 until 1848. Ice harvesting operations began to pollute the pristine water, and the city stopped using it. Luckily, the pond—ninety feet deep at some points—was fed by natural springs, improving the water's quality when the ice harvesters left. With rapid industrialization in the nineteenth century, urban Americans grew concerned about the loss of farmland, forest, and natural open spaces. In 1894 the city purchased the sixty-eight acres around Jamaica Pond to make it part of Frederick Law Olmsted's Emerald Necklace, a series of parks stretching from Franklin Park in Roxbury to the Boston Common. Olmsted took a hands-off design approach here, essentially adding a perimeter walking trail. This photo was taken later that year.

The city demolished the temporary boathouse and built the Jamaica Plain Boathouse and Bandstand in 1913. Also that year, the Children's Museum opened in its original location at Pinebank, or the Perkins Estate, formerly a private mansion overlooking the pond. While Pinebank has fallen into disrepair since the Children's Museum moved to Fort Point Channel in the 1970s, there are actually several mansions on the Jamaicaway, the road snaking along Jamaica Pond. One of them—it has shamrocks cut into the shutters—belonged to James Michael Curley. As for the pond, it has been for decades an urban oasis for boaters, strollers, and fishers (the state wildlife division stocks the pond with salmon). Swimming has been prohibited for years, but there is talk of bringing that back. More or less as Olmsted had hoped, Jamaica Pond is a place where all Bostonians can come to rejuvenate.

Just south of Jamaica Pond and west of Forest Hills, the Arnold Arboretum is another link in Frederick Law Olmsted's network of green spaces. These lands once belonged to Benjamin Bussey, a Revolutionary War veteran and a "scientific farmer" of the early nineteenth century. Bussey bequeathed his rolling hills, filled with a mix of ancient forests and his own experimental plantings, to Harvard University. With another gift left to Harvard by Quaker whaler and abolitionist James Arnold, horticulture professor Charles Sprague Sargent—a cousin of portrait artist John Singer Sargent—organized and directed the new Arnold Arboretum starting in 1872. Sargent worked with Olmsted on a plan whereby Harvard kept charge of the arboretum while turning it over to Boston's parks system in 1882. Here is the arboretum's front gate and headquarters around 1905.

Strolling along the winding trails of the arboretum today, it's almost hard to believe you're in the city. The 265-acre botanical garden features boulders, ponds, meadows, and 6,500 varieties of plants, from redbuds, dogwoods, honeysuckles, lilacs, and azaleas to American maples, Lebanese cedars, and Roman pines. Plant explorer Ernest Wilson brought tree and shrub seeds from climatically appropriate parts of China, Taiwan, Japan, and Korea in the early 1900s, and the results live on here despite the Great Hurricane of 1938, which knocked over more than a thousand trees. The Olmsted- and Sargent-engineered city-university arrangement has allowed scientific research to proceed while providing the public with a relaxing and edifying outdoor refuge. That legacy should endure as parents and school programs expose the next generation to the arboretum's wonders.

A group of Puritans established Dorchester in 1630, independently of—and just months before—John Winthrop and the Massachusetts Bay Company's settlement of Boston to the north. For more than two centuries, Dorchester was essentially a rural New England town, with a few developed clusters surrounded by large tracts of farmland. The Yankee residents governed by town meetings, held in the original First Parish Church on the village green, known as Dorchester Common (later Reverend Allen Park). They built the neoclassical Lyceum Hall

(right) in the 1840s to accommodate larger public meetings as new railroads brought more people and development. Dorchester's first Roman Catholic Masses were held there for Irish immigrants in the 1850s, and it served as a Union army recruiting station during the Civil War. Dorchester merged with Boston in 1870. Horse-drawn streetcar lines brought more Irish, and in 1872 the archdiocese built St. Peter's abutting the green. The Colonial-era First Parish building burned down in 1896; its replacement is seen here four years later.

First Parish Church was soon eclipsed by its new neighbor. St. Peter's became one of Boston's strongest Catholic parishes as the Meeting House Hill area turned almost entirely Irish in the early twentieth century. That paralleled much of Dorchester (or "Dot" for short) after annexation: by World War II, a dozen parishes had been consecrated in the town (and it was still referred to as a town). Well into the 1980s—at least—this was a tight-knit working-class neighborhood where kids attended St. Peter's, started gangs called the Saints or the Red Raiders, organized their own street hockey leagues, and grew up to be cops. Recently, however, declining enrollment has led the scandal-plagued and financially strapped archdiocese to consider closing St. Peter's School. Meanwhile, First Parish, with about sixty members, has to replace its rotted belfry because its steeple was tilting dangerously. The steeple is sitting where the lyceum (demolished in 1955) was. Unchanged from the old photo is the Civil War monument.

Dorchester's population exploded from 12,000 in 1870 to 150,000 in 1920. That required a wee bit of residential construction. It was happening in Roxbury and other new parts of the city, too. For the last third of the nineteenth century, as Sam Bass Warner Jr. details in *Streetcar Suburbs*, speculators and builders subdivided the remaining old farmlands, laid out streets, and put up substantial one- and two-family houses some distance apart from one another. By the early twentieth century, the trend was toward the three-story structures, typified here, that would eventually predominate in residential Boston and Dorchester. Narrow streets lined with narrow lots sprouted detached wooden houses that filled with three (or six) lower-middle-class families each. Between Geneva Avenue and Washington, Dakota Street lay at the fringe of St. Peter's parish, toward the largely Jewish neighborhoods to the west. Despite the presence of the archaic junk collectors' horse-drawn carts, this picture was actually taken in 1956.

Just three years after the old photo was taken, the Boston archdiocese redrew parish lines in order to spread resources evenly across thriving Catholic Dorchester. To lighten the load on St. Peter's, officials shifted Dakota Street and environs into St. Ambrose, near Fields Corner, meaning longtime St. Peter's parishioners could no longer send their kids to St. Peter's School, or marry or be buried by St. Peter's. Residents wrote heartfelt letters to the popular Cardinal Cushing, to no avail. A decade later, the neighborhood was affected by another set of lines drawn on a map: the mortgage-lenders' redlining that hastened white, especially Jewish, flight from Roxbury and parts of Dorchester and Mattapan. Around 7,000 abandoned three-story houses burned in the 1970s, but Boston bounced back from that low point. Many of the houses have been converted into pricey condominiums. Dakota, though, is still an unassuming side street, now in an African American neighborhood.

In the foreground of this photograph from 1887 is Pope's Hill (onetime home of suffragette Lucy Stone). Across Tenean Creek are the tracks of the New York, New Haven and Hartford Railroad. And beyond that, on Barque Warwick Cove, is Commercial Point, long an axis of Dorchester industry. Commercial Point sited a salt works, a chocolate factory, an iron foundry, cod fisheries, and cooper's shops over the course of the nineteenth century. From its wharves in the early 1800s, schooners embarked on trading expeditions in the East Indies, and in the 1830s, whaling ships left on four-year voyages to the Pacific, returning with barrels of sperm oil, and whalebone for jewelry. D. J. Cutter, who took this picture, sold heating oil from Commercial Point. By the 1880s, the Boston Gas Light Company had the biggest presence there—note the large gasometer at the top of this image. Another one lies across Dorchester Bay, on the Calf Pasture (later Columbia Point), at left. That belongs to the competing Bay State Gas Company.

Looking toward the Point from Ronan Park, note the MBTA Red Line tracks (left) along the old New Haven line. Boston Gas became Commercial Point's sole entity by 1900 as smaller shops left for safety reasons. (The Cutter family still runs D. J.'s heating fuel business, now on Freeport Street.) In 1967 and 1969, Boston Gas built two tanks here for liquefied natural gas. The company commissioned artist and former nun Corita Kent to enliven one of the tanks in 1971. Then known for designing the "Love" postage stamp, Kent endeavored to symbolize peace with the now-familiar rainbow of brushstrokes, the largest copyrighted work of art in the world. Aware of her antiwar views, some claimed they saw Ho Chi Minh's profile in the painting. Today, most appreciate the public art on a landmark now owned by National Grid. The current painting is in fact a reproduction, as the original adorned a tank that was dismantled in 1992.

After the Minot family and other colonists settled here, they battled the Wampanoag warriors of Metacomet, also known as "King Philip," for control of the territory. One account even has the Minots' servant girl shoveling hot coal at a warrior's face. The Minot House sat near here until a fire destroyed it in 1874. Adams Street was long known as the Lower Road, or the Lower Road to Milton. William Adams was master of a schoolhouse on the road in the 1840s. (He was also a poet and humorist under the pen name "Oliver Optic.") As late as the 1880s, farmers drove cows to the market this way from pastures along the Neponset River. Eventually, the Irish colonized the territory: St. Ann's was built on Minot Street in 1881, moving to bigger quarters on Neponset Avenue in 1920; St. Brendan's opened in 1933 on Gallivan Boulevard. Here, the business district at the intersection of Adams and Gallivan is seen possibly after the Great Hurricane of 1938.

The former Guay's is still a bakery, now called Greenhills (at right, with the Irish flag, below the Tudor-style house). Next door is Gerard's restaurant and corner store. Open since 1970, that venerable institution draws patrons from all over Boston and the South Shore. Better known nationally, however, is its peer across the street. In 1972 the Eire Pub appeared (disguised as the Bright Red) in the late George V. Higgins's *The Digger's Game*. (Higgins wouldn't be the last local writer to mine Dorchester for material; native "Dot rat" Dennis Lehane's

books have lately brought the neighborhood to the silver screen.) Then, in 1983, wading into traditionally Democratic territory, President Ronald Reagan made an unannounced stop at the Eire, forever putting the blue-collar bar on the map. Later, Mayor Ray Flynn brought candidate Bill Clinton here in 1992. Other visiting pols have included senators John Kerry and Ted Kennedy—and Reagan's son Ron, who (reportedly unlike either his father or Clinton) drained an entire beer.

At the very farthest reaches of Roxbury, along the Sawmill Brook flowing into the Charles River, Unitarian minister George Ripley and his wife, Sophia, bought a farm in 1841, mortgaging it to friend and former Boston mayor Josiah Quincy. There, the couple started a transcendentalist Utopian community called Brook Farm, an experiment in cooperative Christian living. Nathaniel Hawthorne was a member, and Ralph Waldo Emerson a frequent visitor. After a philosophical split, a fire, and a financial lawsuit by Hawthorne, the community dissolved in 1846. The newly incorporated City of Roxbury took over the site and operated it as an almshouse, even in the 1850s (when this photo was taken). At that time, the farm lay beyond its official borders due to West Roxbury's split from Roxbury out of concern over preserving its pastoral character.

All that is left of the Brook Farm complex today is "the Hive," the farmhouse that predates the Ripleys' purchase. During the Civil War, the farm served as a training camp for the Second Massachusetts Infantry. West Roxbury's "independence" was brief. After Roxbury voted for annexation to Boston in 1868, the growing populace of West Roxbury (then encompassing Jamaica Plain and Roslindale) decided to follow, in 1874. Railroads and streetcar lines drew West Roxbury closer to Boston, and it became a dense suburban neighborhood of one- and two-family homes. A Yankee holdout into the 1930s, the district was by the end of the century largely Irish and Greek, with a large number of teachers, firefighters, police, and other city workers. Kevin White, mayor of Boston from 1967 to 1983, was from "Westie." Well away from busy Centre Street, the Brook Farm National Historic Site sits in a wooded nature preserve on the Charles that includes the successful new Millennium Park, once a trash heap.